BEYOND ONTOLOGICAL BLACKNESS

———————

· VICTOR ANDERSON ·

BEYOND ONTOLOGICAL BLACKNESS

AN ESSAY ON

African American Religious and Cultural Criticism

· · ·

CONTINUUM · NEW YORK

1999

The Continuum Publishing Company
370 Lexington Avenue
New York, NY 10017

Printed in the United States of America

Library of Congress Cataloging-in-Publication Data

Anderson, Victor. 1955–
   Beyond ontological blackness : an essay on African-American religious and
cultural criticism / Victor Anderson. p. cm.
   Includes bibliographical references and index.
   ISBN 0–8264–1152–5 (pbk)
   1. Afro-Americans—Religion. 2. Black theology—Controversial
literature. 3. Womanist theology—Controversial literature. 4. Afro-Americans—
Race identity. 5. United States—Civilization—20th century. 6. United States—
Race relations. 7. United States—Moral conditions. 8. United States—Church
history—20th century. I. Title.
BR563.N2A53 1995   95–32401
305.896′073—dc20   CIP

In memory of my departed loved ones
who continue to intercede on my behalf.

■　■　■

To my mother, Flora Helen Anderson,
a religious critic who rejects idolatry
wherever it is found and who
sees possibilities for hope
in the darkest times.

CONTENTS

■ ■ ■

ACKNOWLEDGMENTS

∎ ∎ ∎

As always, I am grateful for the rigorous intellectual discipline afforded me at Princeton University by my teachers Jeffrey L. Stout, Malcolm Diamond, Victor Preller, and Cornel West. Each one will find himself echoed throughout this book. I am thankful to friends who encouraged my work and made helpful suggestions for my thinking through many of its issues. I owe thanks to Professors Eugene Sutton, William D. Hart, Peter J. Paris, and Marcia Riggs who all read a prior draft. A special thanks to Dr. Mark Tazelaar whose philosophical work on Habermas, Foucault, Deridda, and Blumenberg afforded me not only opportunity for critical thinking but also many hours of pleasurable debate. Dr. Forrest Harris, dean and director of the Kelly Miller Smith Institute for the Study of the Black Church at Vanderbilt University, has been a most formidable interlocutor, as have several of my graduate students: Christine Caron, Charles Bryan Owen, and Chandra Taylor-Smith. To Cynthia Eller and Evander Lomke, whose editorial wisdom guided me to think better and more clearly about the matters of this book, I am grateful. As always my family: my mother, Flora Anderson, sisters (Victoria, Deborah, Paulete, Valentine, Crystal, Diane, Delores, and Barbara), nieces and nephews, and Jac remain key sources of inspiration for my ongoing work.

Many of my students at Vanderbilt University have endured much while I was preparing this essay. Courses I taught at Vanderbilt University Divinity School and the Graduate Department of Religion in ethics in theological perspective, African American political theology, twentieth-century North Atlantic ethics, ethics and society, and religion and critical theory were convenient fields for clarifying many of the interests expressed in this book. I thank my students for their patience and conversations. Finally, I am thankful to Howard Harrod and Dean Joseph C. Hough, Jr., my colleagues in Religion, Ethics and Society, for their encouragement and wisdom.

INTRODUCTION

■ ■ ■

Beyond Ontological Blackness examines the ways that racial discourse operates rhetorically in African American cultural and religious thought. The disclosure of the ways that race is reified—i.e., treated as if it objectively exists independent of historically contingent factors and subjective intentions—in the writings of historical and contemporary African American cultural and religious thinkers is the *first* theme of the book. Throughout this book, I describe this tendency toward racial reification as *ontological blackness*. Ontological blackness is a covering term that connotes categorical, essentialist, and representational languages depicting black life and experience. In contrast to ontological blackness, I commend the racial discourse that bell hooks, a leading contemporary African American cultural critic, calls "postmodern blackness" (1990, 23ff.).

Postmodern blackness recognizes the permanency of race as an effective category in identity formation. However, it also recognizes that black identities are continually being reconstituted as African Americans inhabit widely differentiated social spaces and communities of moral discourse. African American life and experience occur in differentiated socio-economic spaces along divisions of education, income, and occupations. And the variety of communities of moral discourse that influence black life and experience may include churches, temples, mosques, and many non-religious voluntary organizations (Sigelman and Welch, 1991, 16ff.). In these multiple sites, African Americans are continuously negotiating the various languages of race, class, gender, and sexuality. Explicating these languages requires historical research and analysis of the ways that African Americans constitute and negotiate their identities under changing social conditions.

Race linguistically designates ethnic groups of human beings. Sometimes these groups are identified by nationalities, families, or languages (Omi and Winant, 1995, 4). Race has here an accidental quality rather than a formal status. For that persons belong to specific ethnic groups has to do with the historical development of particular human communities, their encounters with other human communities, and the economic conditions under which these communities propagate themselves. This use of race is one that is likely to guide cultural anthropologists, and it is central to the claims that I make for the critical study of race throughout this book. However, in many of the cultural studies that I examine, mostly philosophical and theological ones, race is often regarded as a topic in metaphysical ontology. In metaphysical ontology, race denotes essential properties (essences), such that to lack any one property renders one a member of a pseudospecies.

According to Erik Erikson, the idea of *pseudospecies* is connected with group identity formation (1968, 41–42). As human groups construct their identities in relation to other animal groups, they develop categorical ways of solidifying their cultural and social identities. One way that they reassure their social and cultural identities is by defining them in terms of positive qualities that they wish to affirm while projecting negative ones onto *others,* rendering *others* false instances of the species. Pseudospecies is the name Erikson gives for this *othering* activity. Erikson warns that while such activities appear to be present throughout almost every group that we know of, "the pseudospecies . . . is one of the more sinister aspects of all group identity" (1968, 42). For according to Erikson, "there are also 'pseudo' aspects in all identity which endanger the individual" (42).

Race is one classification under which human group differentiation occurs. In this book, I am interested in the ways that race determines black identity in African American cultural philosophy and theology. The *second* theme of the book is to make problematic the historic representational functions that race language has had in these cultural studies. In the West, racial representation is closely identified with the Western aesthetic category of genius. (In chapter 4, I give an extensive account of the idea of genius in European aesthetic theory.) In their attempts to give ideological justification for the imperialist ethos that inaugurated the age of Europe, European intellectuals defined their age and themselves as heroic, epochal, and exhibiting racial genius.

Comparatively speaking, then, this racial aesthetic renders the other (non-Europeans) a false species, lacking in essential properties which make European genius representative of universal human genius. The *third* theme is that the cult of European genius, with its essentially heroic, epochal, and culture-advancing qualities, has likewise determined how African Americans represent themselves as the mirror of European genius: ontological blackness signifies the blackness that whiteness created.

Beyond Ontological Blackness focuses on *the cult of black heroic genius.* I use the word *cult* here to designate dispositions of devotion, loyalty, and admiration for racial categories and the essentialized principles that determine black identity. And racial genius refers to the exceptional, sometimes essentialized cultural qualities, that positively represent the racial group in the action of at least one of the group's members. Insofar as the one member's actions are said to represent the genius of the group (whether that member is a Sojouner Truth, a Marian Anderson, a Dr. Martin Luther King, Jr., a Malcolm X, a Michael Jordan, or a Jessye Norman) that member also exhibits the heroic qualities of the race. Of course, as the notion of pseudospecies shows, such racial reasoning can also give way to negative categorical judgments about the race. Therefore, ontological blackness entails a type of categorical racial reasoning and a black aesthetic—a collective racial consciousness expressive and representational of African American genius.

Ontological blackness is a philosophy of racial consciousness. It is governed by dialectical matrices that existentially structure African Americans' self-conscious perceptions of black life. Under ontological blackness, the conscious lives of blacks are experienced as bound by unresolved binary dialectics of slavery and freedom, negro and citizen, insider and outsider, black and white, struggle and survival. However, such binary polarities admit no possibility of transcendence or mediation. Negatively, each pole is not so determinant that one pole is canceled out by the other. To be sure, negation occurs but in the same way as negative (-A) anticipates and represents in its own internal meaning positive (+A). Positively, in these racial polarities, the one pole is reflected or mirrored by the other in the same way that not (-A) = (+A). Whether one accents the negative or positive qualities of racial polarization (negation or mirroring), the representational intentions of these binary dialectics remain untranscended. The dialectical structure of ontological blackness provides a unity of representational intentions in cultural studies. And W. E. B. Du Bois's double-consciousness depiction of black existence has come to epitomize the existential determinants of black self-consciousness. These alienated forms of black consciousness have been categorically defined in African American cultural studies as: The Negro Problem, The Color Line, Black Experience, Black Power, The Veil of Blackness, Black Radicalism, and most recently, The Black Sacred Cosmos.

There is a close connection between ontological blackness and religion. Ontological blackness signifies the totality of black existence, a binding together of black life and experience. In its root, *religio,* religion denotes tying together, fastening behind, and binding together. Ontological blackness renders black life and experience a totality. It is a totality that takes narrative formations that emphasize the heroic capacities of African Americans to transcend individuality and personality in the name of black communal survival. In these survivalist narratives, the black community is often represented as surviving under unprecedented struggle by the development of a revolutionary consciousness that is itself representational of authentic black consciousness. This book explores the ways that devotion to ontological blackness, its categories and its interests in racial solidarity, loyalty, and authenticity, conceals, subjugates, and calls into question African Americans' interests in fulfilled individuality.

As a critic of the categorical and representational functions of ontological blackness, I suggest that there are good critical reasons for pressing beyond its centrality in black cultural studies. First, in its categorical and representational functions, ontological blackness distorts far too much of the conditions of African American life and experience in the United States. African American life and experience are structured by dispersed and not always commensurable interests of class, gender, sexual differentials, and race.

Therefore, racial identity is not total, although it is always present. From a religious point of view, when race is made total, then ontological blackness is idolatrous, approaching racial henotheism. As a religious critic whose religious and moral sensibilities are derived from a radical monotheistic faith, I find myself at odds with such a cultural idolatry.

A second warrant for pressing beyond ontological blackness is that the idea is incommensurable with the demand for a new cultural politics of black identity that meaningfully relates to the conditions of postmodern North American life. A list of African American literary and cultural critics calling for a new politics of black identity includes Cornel West, bell hooks, Toni Morrison, Alice Walker, Henry Lewis Gates, Jr., Houston Baker, Jr., Darlene Clark Hine, Wilson J. Moses, Michael Dyson, and Joe Wood. The new cultural politics of difference takes seriously the ways that ontological blackness alienates African Americans who pursue genuine interests in personal fulfillment along class, gender, ethnic, and sexual differentials. The *fourth* theme governing this book is that those racial discourses that derive their legitimacy from ontological blackness are at odds with contemporary postmodern black life.

Beyond Ontological Blackness does not reject all those prior historical projects, which responded to the pressing problems and crises of black life, and were provoked by the criminal history of modern racism. Nor does *beyond* mean the *negation* of blacks' interest in the development and fulfillment of positive African American communities throughout the United States. This book owes an unpayable debt to the intellectual labors of past and contemporary African American artists and intellectuals who responded to the demonic influences of modern racism in American life and culture.

In chapter 2, I give a brief genealogy of modern racism in terms of categorical racism and white racial ideology. Both discourses were developed from the Enlightenment and Romantic aesthetics where race emerged as both a criterion of cultural differentiation (categorical racism) and a criterion for excluding blacks from the freedoms of democracy (white racial ideology).

I also discuss how modern racism rendered African American cultural philosophy preoccupied with racial apologetics. From David Walker, Booker T. Washington, W. E. B. Du Bois, and Marcus Garvey to the black theology project (discussed in chapter 3), African American cultural philosophy and theology responded to modern racism by depicting the racial genius of blacks as entailed in the marks of European genius. The argument of chapters 2 and 3, then, is that modern racism (its defining categories of categorical racism and white racial ideology) returns in African American cultural studies as a reversal.

Racial identity categorically binds together black life, and ideologically legitimizes and authenticates the various cultural activities of African Americans—whether in cultural philosophy or black theology. Unfortunately, the need among African Americans to promote a positive racial community has too often taken binary dialectical formation against individuality. In the dialectic of community and individuality, where community is totalized, blacks who pursue goods that contribute to their fulfillment as individuals (whether selecting marriage partners, exercising the freedom of movement, acting on gay and lesbian preferences, or choosing political parties) often find themselves ostracized and their cultural fulfillment repressed by an ontological blackness. My attempt is not to negate but to displace, decenter, and transcend the determinative transactions and practices of ontological blackness over black life and experience.

Pressing beyond ontological blackness, chapter 4 explores the genealogy of heroic racial aesthetics in Western thought and juxtaposes it to the Nietzschean grotesque aesthetic. I regard the grotesque aesthetic as a morally credible source for reconfiguring African American religious and cultural criticism. The grotesque aesthetic holds in tension the ambiguities between attraction and repulsion, and exposes both the light and dark sides of culture. It recognizes that things can be otherwise than how they appear. Ambiguity and difference constitute the normative gaze of the grotesque figure. The *fifth* theme of the book is that the grotesque aesthetic adequately undergirds the rationality of difference that is proposed in the new literary critiques of ontological blackness.

However, pressing beyond ontological blackness to a new cultural politics of difference requires more than aesthetic criticism. According to Adolf Reed, bell hooks, and Cornel West, negotiating the new cultural politics of difference requires that African American cultural and religious critics disclose and subvert those cultural institutions and practices that undermine the cultural fulfillment of African Americans within a democratic form of life. It also requires that critics support those institutions and practices that assure more democracy.

The aims of cultural criticism, as I develop it in chapter 1, are (a) to describe the patterns of social life that intend human fulfillment, (b) to criticize those cultural activities that undermine human fulfillment, and (c) to advance those cultural activities that increase human fulfillment. Cultural criticism, at its best, will be both enlightening and emancipatory. It will be enlightening about the ways that our societies and cultural activities condition possibilities for the fulfillment of basic human needs and subjective goods. It will also be enlightening about the ways that our societies and cultural activities often undermine cultural fulfillment. It will be emancipatory insofar as it is not only driven by descriptive and pejorative critiques of culture but also advances and supports those cultural activities that increase human and cultural fulfillment. The religious functions of cultural criticism contribute an unrelenting iconoclastic rigor that is oppositional to proposed totalities of cultural life that undermine human and cultural fulfillment.

Another religious function of cultural criticism is a utopian hope that sees possibilities for human flourishing where the threat of nihilism seems pervasive over postmodern North American culture. The form of cultural and religious criticism that I propose is (a) iconoclastic and utopian, (b) derived from the sociological tradition and critical theory, (c) is in the service of cultural criticism, and (d) is aggressive about making cultural fulfillment the defining category of African American cultural and religious criticism. That the legitimacy of African American cultural and religious criticism should be grounded on cultural fulfillment is the *sixth* governing theme of this book.

In this book, I am not content with only providing a descriptively enlightening account of the totalizing reification of race in African American cultural studies. Nor am I content with pointing out dead ends to effective criticism in African American cultural and religious thought. My positive aim is to explicate the conditions for self-critical discourse among African Americans that are commensurable with the demands of a politics of black identity that exonerates the contributions of class, gender, and sexual difference to positive black identities. I have written this book in order to clear a path for an African American public theology that has cultural fulfillment as the content of liberation and whose justifications are predicated on a new politics of black identity. Rather than overburdening the chapters with technical footnotes, I have placed, at the end of the book, a brief annotated bibliography that the reader may consult. The books and articles listed in Works Cited are also representative of sources that inform the composition of this book.

one

THE RELIGIOUS FUNCTIONS OF
CULTURAL CRITICISM

■ ■ ■

What is cultural and religious criticism? How are they related to African American religious thought? These questions are addressed in this chapter. The first section examines the idea of cultural criticism in general. Cultural criticism is an intellectual activity that analyzes the structural and expressive ways that human groups satisfy basic human needs and subjective goods. It examines the ways that distorted communication at various institutional levels undermines the satisfaction of these goods. It discloses the ways that human cultural activities can enter into legitimation crises. And it commends those activities by which persons can transcend social crisis and fulfill their cultural activities.

Cultural criticism, at its best, will be both culturally enlightening and emancipatory. It will not only point out the dark sides of culture, but will also advance public languages that are oriented toward cultural fulfillment.

The second section explicates the religious functions of cultural criticism. In religious criticism, the enlightening and emancipatory intentions of cultural criticism are conceived iconoclastically. Religious criticism rejects the totalization of what is particular and centers public discourse on causes or loyalties that transcend every particularity. In its iconoclastic and utopian modes, religious criticism is a function of cultural criticism. These religious functions of cultural criticism are discussed in relation to the recent postmodern debates about secular and religious criticism.

The last section examines select writings of two African American religious critics, Howard Thurman (1900–1981) and Cornel West (1953–). These writers are examined as exemplary religious critics. Each in his own way and under different contexts displays the dual dimensions of cultural and religious criticism. Each critic names and unmasks demonic powers that vitiate cultural fulfillment among African Americans. Each does so in the name of some transcendent cause and loyalty (beloved community or radical democracy) around which African Americans may center their hopes of cultural fulfillment.

EXPLICATING CULTURAL CRITICISM

Cultural criticism is a confused idea, and it means different things to different thinkers. To some, cultural criticism describes activities that constitute a particular human form of life. To others, cultural criticism proposes ways in which the real interests of persons and their social aspirations are advanced. Therefore, cultural criticism can be both descriptive (insofar as it describes human activities) and constructive (insofar as it commends human activities worthy of pursuing in the interest of cultural fulfillment). I think that it is best to understand cultural criticism by looking at its two defining aspects: social analysis and the critique of ideology.

Culture is formally a system of human practices that constitute human societies. Culture is a system of interconnected and interfunctional spheres of human activity. These spheres include economic, political, moral, religious, artistic, and linguistic activities. It is important to keep in mind that these various cultural spheres do not exist independent of each other. They are socially interconnected and mutually reassuring. However, we inhabit an intellectual climate in which many intellectuals feel repulsed by any talk of social systems or life-worlds (Jameson, 1991, xi). Many are more inclined to talk about the ways that our various cultural spheres no longer appear socially interconnected and reinforcing of supposed universal purposes or common goods and interests.

A thinker such as Alasdair MacIntyre stresses the ways in which contemporary north Atlantic societies are riddled by fragility. Mass societies are left without much hope of resolving internal conflicts between their various social institutions. MacIntyre writes:

> One of the most striking facts about modern political orders is that they lack institutionalized forums within which these fundamental disagreements can be systematically explored and charted, let alone there being any attempt made to resolve them. The facts of disagreement themselves frequently go unacknowledged, disguised by a rhetoric of consensus. And when on some single, if complex issue, as in the struggle over the Vietnam war or in the debates over abortion, the illusions of consensus on questions of justice and practical rationality are for the moment fractured, the expression of radical disagreement is institutionalized in such a way as to abstract that single issue from those background contexts of different and incompatible beliefs from which such disagreements arise. This serves to prevent, so far as is possible, debate extending to the fundamental principles which inform those background beliefs.
>
> Private citizens are thus for the most part left to their own devices in these matters. (1988, 2–3)

MacIntyre's point is that talk about systems of social interconnectedness or integration seems hard to justify given the incommensurability and disequilibrium between our cultural practices. Cultural fragility makes any talk about systems of unified common interests or consensus about common goods, ends, and purposes seem absurd. Therefore, advancing a theory of cultural criticism that is predicated on social system theories appears dubious to many intellectuals.

I do not share MacIntyre's pessimism. Cultural criticism presupposes that constellations of human actions are susceptible to analysis. Analysis suggests that analogical correlations obtain among distinct phenomena. If our various social spheres do not exist isolated and unrelated to each other, then we cannot only compare the distinct activities that constitute a culture (labor, family, clans, castes, markets, religion, and the like), but we can also analyze these distinct activities in relation to some entailing social theory (civic republicanism, national socialism, communism, or fascism) and method (analytic, typological, comparative, historical, hermeneutic, deconstructive, and so forth). Cultural criticism therefore is not opposed to social theory or method.

To regard culture as a system or webs of human social actions is to be theoretically and methodologically committed to an organic account of culture. Organic accounts of culture reject classical dichotomies of culture between the real and the ephemeral, or phenomena and epiphenomena. Such an organic understanding of culture is clearly put forward in Clifford Geertz's semiotic account of cultural analysis:

> The concept of culture I espouse . . . is essentially a semiotic one. Believing, with Max Weber, that man is an animal suspended in webs of significance he himself has spun, I take culture to be those webs, and the analysis of it to be therefore not an experimental science in search of law but an interpretative one in search of meaning. It is explication I am after, construing social expressions on their surface enigmatical. (Geertz, 1973, 5)

Three aspects of Geertz's definition of culture are instructive for understanding cultural criticism: (a) the social activities constitutive of culture are semiotic, (b) these activities are human actions and exhibit human intentions, and (c) although cultures may be enigmatic, they are nevertheless open to interpretation and analysis.

The social phenomenologists Schutz and Luckmann offer an organic account of these three Geertzian moments in cultural analysis. Like Geertz, they reject any dichotomies of culture in terms of subjectivity versus materialism or phenomena versus epiphenomena. Their organic account of cultural analysis emphasizes intersubjective communication and privileges the *natural attitude*. I quote them at length:

> In the natural attitude of everyday life the following is taken for granted without question: (a) the corporeal existence of other men; (b) that these bodies are endowed with consciousness essentially similar to my own; (c) that the things of the outer world included in my environs and that of my fellow-men are the same for us and have the same meaning; (d) that I can enter into interrelations and reciprocal actions with my fellow-men; (e) that I can make myself understood to them (which follow from the preceding assumptions); (f) that a stratified social and cultural world is historically pregiven as a frame of reference for me and my fellow-men, indeed in a manner as taken for granted as the "natural world"; (g) that therefore the situation in which I find myself at any moment is only to a small extent purely created by me.
>
> The everyday reality of the life-world includes, therefore, not only the "nature" experienced by me but also the social (and therefore the cultural) world in which I find myself; the life-world is not created out of the merely material objects and events which I encounter in my environment. Certainly these are together one component of my surrounding world; nevertheless, there also belong to this all the meaning-strata which transform natural things into cultural

objects, human bodies into fellow-men, and the movements of fellow-men into acts, gestures, and communications. (1973, 5)

The organic account of cultural analysis, advanced by Geertz, Schutz, and Luckmann, owes a debt to the pragmatic social theory of George Herbert Mead. According to Mead, culture is a reflexive, integrative system of purposive activity. And culture is a projection of the ends and values that societies intend in their purposive activities (Mead, 1932, 90; 1964, 248–66). Therefore, Mead's pragmatic social theory does not try to shield from scrutiny the constellation of values commended in our various and sometimes conflicting ideologies, whether in theology, ethics, or cultural philosophy. Rather, Mead regarded the human social actions that constitute a culture as being both formative and expressive of human needs and interests (Mead, 1932, 69, 74, 82–87).

The formative and expressive aspects of culture are disclosed in human activities and practiced in differentiated social spaces. These differentiated spaces can range from simple to very complex matrices such as clans and families, religions and societies, classes and castes, labor and markets, and states and governments. Notwithstanding how complex social differentiation may be, cultural integrity obtains insofar as a culture can achieve the successful satisfaction of the basic categorical human needs of which persons seek fulfillment through their various social activities. Such categorical needs include those goods that are minimally necessary for sustaining biological life: life, safety, work, leisure, knowledge, and the like.

Cultural integrity also obtains insofar as communicative forms of action satisfy the reflexive goods that persons require for assuring subjective meaning and alleviating alienation. Such goods may include friendship, peace of mind, integrity of conscience, spiritual meaning, and so forth. (Habermas, 1989, 135–48; Finnis, 1992, 99–289; Grisez and Shaw, 1991, 54–56). This integration of human social activity with the satisfaction of categorical and reflexive human goóds is referred to throughout this book as *cultural fulfillment.*

Thus far my account of cultural criticism says far more about culture than it says about criticism. Cultural criticism is concerned with the processes of successful cultural fulfillment and the social conditions under which cultural fulfillment can be either achieved or undermined in pluralist societies. Because cultural criticism is concerned with explicating the processes and conditions under which cultural fulfillment is either satisfied or frustrated, it is necessarily descriptive. However, cultural criticism is not likely to be very emancipatory if it is only oriented toward descriptive social analysis. It not only has social practices as the object of critique, but it is also concerned with the critique of ideology.

Ideological criticism exhibits three tendencies which Raymond Geuss (1981) categorizes as descriptive, pejorative, and positive. In the descriptive mode, according to Geuss, ideological criticism focuses on the "concepts [societies] use, the attitudes and psychological dispositions they exhibit, their motives, desires, values, predilections, works of art, religious rituals, gestures, etc." (5). In the pejorative mode, the task of ideological criticism is to unmask the illusionary and falsifying ways that cultural activities deny the real interests of persons (12–22). This pejorative mode of ideological criticism is suggested in the Marxian notion of false consciousness and the Freudian notion of illusionary consciousness. Ideological criticism in the positive mode engages the constructive interests of the critic. It admits into cultural criticism the proactive posture of the critic of culture.

The critic posits an ideology that he or she believes will best reassure and satisfy a culture's real interests (22–26). Under the positive mode, ideology refers to a cultural symbol-system, guiding human communities politically, rendering ambiguous social relations meaningful, and mapping social problems and contexts for the purpose of establishing a common moral conscience, says Rejai (1973, 558; compare Geertz, 1964). When the critique of ideology is a function of cultural criticism, it contributes to a reflexive mode of discourse by which persons explain themselves to themselves and discern, affirm, and promote those practices that fulfill their cultural ends and purposes.

Cultural criticism does not merely describe the dark sides of social activity, but it resists the temptation toward cynicism by reasserting and affirming creative possibilities for human flourishing. Cultural criticism is constructive when it sees among the moral ruins of our contemporary societies possibilities for human flourishing and possibilities for realizing our political, social, and spiritual ideals. Such possibilities make cultural transcendence an essential aspect of cultural criticism.

The stereoscopic gaze that "brings social practices and institutions, internal and external goods into focus at the same time" is the normative gaze of the cultural critic, says Jeffrey L. Stout (1988, 279). This means that the cultural critic keeps both eyes open on the human condition. From this perspective, perhaps every culture exhibits conditions in which the categorical and reflexive goods persons require for human flourishing are threatened and denied by distorted activities within society. However, where human activities genuinely achieve reflexive integration of categorical and subjective goods within society, the debilitating and oppressive formations of culture operationalized in racism, classism, sexism, and homophobia cannot be regarded as totalities. In this book, the stereoscopic view of cultural criticism is commended as an appropriate basis for African American religious criticism. In the following section, I discuss the religious aspects of cultural criticism in relation to secular criticism.

RELIGIOUS ASPECTS OF CULTURAL CRITICISM

As social analysis and the critique of ideology, cultural criticism is a context for religious criticism. Religious criticism is a viable aspect of cultural criticism. However, it is not theology except in a broad or loosely defined sense. Conversely, theology is not religious criticism, except in the very mitigated sense that all theologians who possess faith in some object that they find worthy of ultimate devotion can be said to be religious. However, the consensus among many noted theologians is that the integrity of theology as a vocation requires more than loose generalities about religious languages and dispositions (Jennings, 1985).

According to Harvard theologian Gordon Kaufman, theology requires the explication of a particular conceptual scheme if it is to differentiate its defining activities from the philosophy of religions (Kaufman, 1993, 70ff.). Theology as a vocation tends to be associated with at least two normative and specific tasks, which may be (but need not be) required of religious criticism. "A theological system is supposed to satisfy two basic needs," says Paul Tillich. It is "the statement of the truth of the Christian message and the interpretation of this truth for every new generation" (Tillich, 1967, 3). Tillich explains that "theology is the methodological interpretation of the contents of the Christian faith" (15).

When theology is a methodological function of the Christian church its task is to integrate internally the variety of religious beliefs and practices held and carried out by its members. Theology reflexively integrates the differences of its members' beliefs under governing categories, which isolate object(s) of ultimate concern, devotion, and loyalty. They give meaning to members' individual practices in light of communal beliefs and liturgical practices. Theology as a vocation serves a particular religious community. When it is successful, it reassures the community's self-understanding as a religious community.

In the form of religious criticism that I defend, the relation between the religious critic and theology is organic and not vocational. The religious critic is organically related to particular beliefs and moral vocabularies that define religious communities. And the critic may bring his or her own faith to bear on the critique of culture. Insights, prejudices, fears, anxieties, hostilities, affirmations, and ground motives, which the critic acquires by participation in a religious community, are all viable sources for religious criticism. However, religious criticism as an aspect of cultural criticism is not strictly justified in terms of ecclesiastical affiliation; neither does its legitimacy depend on whether the belief systems (Catholic, Protestant, Muslim, traditional, and the like) with which the critic identifies are internally satisfying. The integrity of religious criticism depends on whether the religious practices critics commend genuinely contribute to or undermine the processes and possibilities for cultural fulfillment.

In religious criticism, it is important to stress that it is culture itself that is the subject of critique. However, there are some postmodern cultural critics who want to separate cultural criticism from religious criticism altogether and exorcise the religious from cultural criticism by means of a thoroughgoing postmodern form of secular criticism.

Postmodern is a notion that is still developing among cultural critics (Lyotard, 1984, 1992; Jameson, 1991; Huyssen, 1986). I use it to suggest that the historical and traditional sources of Western culture are in today's context of inquiry caught in a crisis of legitimation. These traditional sources allowed European intellectuals to construct comparative judgments that distinguished and justified the European cult of genius from others. The two sources that have been most effective historically in sustaining the legitimacy of Western culture are the Greco-Roman humanist tradition and the Christian theological tradition. If not the whole, much of the problem of legitimacy in the modern age is shaped by reading these traditional sources of cultural legitimation in terms of negative dialectics. Negative dialectics is an oppositional form of reasoning by which we see discourse moving in competitive, antithetical, and hierarchial histories, each contending for intellectual ascendancy. In the twentieth century, such negative dialectics have been subsumed under the category of secularization.

According to Blumenberg (1983), secularization theories tend to explain the rise of modern critical thought in terms of a transference of ideas from philosophical and religious traditions of antiquities to commensurable categories that are determinative of modern thought. When such a transference happens, then the legitimacy of those prior systems of thought weakens or erodes. Blumenberg also suggests that sometimes secularization occurs in terms of negation, a cancelation of the ideas that constitute a prior philosophical and religious tradition by accepting as normative antithetical tenants of another system of thought (1983, 37–51). The crisis of Western culture is accounted for as the result of the progressive secularization (either by usurpation or negation) of the sources of Western cultural traditions by the ascendancy of some oppositional and exclusive counter-discourse.

The *scientization* discourse (proposed by philosophers such as Auguste Comte and John Stuart Mill) approaches secularization by usurpation, while critical theory (such as that of Karl Marx) approaches secularization by negation. Common to both usurpation and negation secularization theories is not only a linear conception of intellectual history, but a presumption that intellectual crises are historically and normatively motivated by exclusionary or oppositional practices.

Philosophers from Martin Heidegger to Richard Rorty suggest that, when metaphysics and truth are exploded by secularization, there must occur a transfiguration in our thinking. Instead of showing the divine in the worldly, philosophers who want a hearing today are virtually required to show that the divine is worldly and that what parades as religious objectivity is itself permeated through and through by textuality. In a summary statement, Rorty writes:

> I can crudely sum up the story which historians like Blumenberg tell by saying that once upon a time we felt a need to worship something which lay beyond the visible world. Beginning in the seventeenth century we tried to substitute

a love of truth for a love of God, treating the world described by science as a quasi divinity. Beginning at the end of the eighteenth century we tried to substitute a love of ourselves for a love of scientific truth, a worship of our own deep spiritual or poetic nature, treated as one more quasi divinity.

The line of thought common to Blumenberg, Nietzsche, Freud, and Davidson suggests that we try to get to the point where we no longer worship *anything*, where we treat *nothing* as a quasi divinity, where we treat *everything*—our language, our conscience, our community—as a product of time and chance. To reach this point would be in Freud's words, to "treat chance as worthy of determining our fate." (Rorty, 1989, 22; Rorty's emphasis)

A thinker like Rorty therefore proposes a reduction of philosophy to edifying discourse. However, a critic such as Edward Said argues that even among those philosophers who argue for cultural criticism as edifying discourse, their cultural criticism is only connotatively *criticism* because such projects have not escaped the antinomies of religious criticism. Said argues that in these edifying discourses, criticism has not achieved its oppositional intentions as a counter-discourse to religious criticism: "How their discourse can once again collectively become a truly secular enterprise, it seems to me, is the most serious question critics can be asking one another," says Said (1983, 292).

Said concludes *The World, the Text, and the Critic* (1983) with a postscript entitled "Religious Criticism." He summarizes the constitutive dialectics that characterize the production and transmission of Western literary culture. His basic opposition is between the *religious* and the *secular*. The secular is a descriptive note signifying the idea of *worldliness*. It is the recognition that textuality is not merely anticipated in the historical circumstances that border human experience (indeed, as if it were a product to be formed rather than an action that is always manifest in our cultural practices). Rather, textuality adequately characterizes the worldliness that elucidates the meaning of culture itself. It signals both the push and pull of cultural productivity.

Contrasted to secular criticism, religious criticism is oppositional to secular discourse. For Said, the religious signals (a) the privatization of spiritual ends, other-worldliness, epistemological certainty in morals, (b) the dogmatism in group solidarity and communal belonging, and (c) the cultural products and institutions whose purposes are to perpetuate successfully the religious intentions of Western culture. A paragraph from Said drives home the point:

> The idea of the Orient, very much like the idea of the West that is its polar opposite, has functioned as an inhibition on what I have been calling secular criticism. Orientalism is the discourse derived from and dependent on "the Orient." To say of such grand ideas and their discourse that they have something in common with religious discourse is to say that each serves as an agent of closure, shutting off human investigation, criticism, and effort in deference to the authority of the more-than-human, the supernatural, the other worldly. Like culture, religion therefore furnishes us with systems of authority and with canons of order whose regular effect is either to compel subservience or to gain adherents. This in turn gives rise to organized collective passions whose social and intellectual results are often disastrous. The persistence of these and other religious-cultural effects testifies amply to what seem to be necessary features of human life, the need for certainty, group solidarity, and a sense of communal belonging. Sometimes of course these things are beneficial. Still it is true that what a secular attitude enables—a sense of history and of human production, along with a healthy skepticism about the various official idols venerated by culture and by system—is diminished, if not eliminated, by appeals to what cannot be thought through and explained, except by consensus and appeals to authority. (290)

Said sees religious intentions as not necessarily or uniquely expressed in religions and theology. As a cultural motive, the religious is wide open to other domains and can be seen wherever we see the tendency for "the secure protection of systems of belief (however peculiar those may be) and not for critical activity or consciousness" (292). Said's aims are to promote a form of secular criticism that eschews the temptations of religiosity, whether in politics, literary criticism, or morals. He envisions a form of critical theory that will complete the functions of secularization and rob even culture itself of totalizing possibilities.

Being both an aesthetic and moral signifier, Said argues that culture exhibits duplicity. As an aesthetic concept, culture denotes expressive aspects of human activity. Such activities as art, handicraft, music, literature, and the human studies (history, philology, sociology, ethnography, and so forth) contribute to the ways that human beings describe and represent themselves to themselves (Said, 1993, xii). According to Said, culture in its aesthetic or expressive functions (in art, narratives, and so forth), especially the culture of imperialism, justifies Western colonization by inventing the *other* as exotic. However, this is not to say that the expressive practices of the exotic *other* do not work as forms of resistance against the culture of imperialism. For narratives "also become the method colonized people use to assert their own identity and the existence of their own history" (1993, xii). Here, culture conditions possibilities for both colonization and resistance.

Culture also has a moral function that "includes a refining and elevating element, each society's reservoir of the best that has been known and thought" (1993, xiii). With this cultural reserve, we achieve social transcendence from the everyday brutalities of our social practices and the various aspects of our social action are united into a grand identity:

> You read Dante and Shakespeare in order to keep up with
> the best that was thought and known, and also to see your-

self, your people, society, and tradition in their best lights. In time, culture comes to be associated, often aggressively, with the nation or the state; this differentiates "us" from "them," almost always with some degree of xenophobia. Culture in this sense is a source of identity, and a rather combative one at that, as we see in recent "returns" to culture and tradition. These "returns" accompany rigorous codes of intellectual and moral behavior that are opposed to the permissiveness associated with such relatively liberal philosophies as multiculturalism and hybridity. In the formally colonized world, these "returns" have produced varieties of religious and nationalist fundamentalism. (1993, xiii)

In this quote, the moral function of culture also reveals a doubling. Moral identity is required for the social integration of our practices. But when the moral functions of culture are totalized, the moral *us* is distinguished from the exotic *them,* and the critical possibilities of culture are subverted by the idolatry of pseudospecies narratives. Both in its aesthetic and moral functions, Said insists that culture remains a religious idea. And the function of secular criticism is to exorcise the religious from cultural criticism.

According to Blumenberg (1983), when secularization theories such as Said's are used polemically and exclusively to negate the traditional sources and insights of philosophy and religious thought, they tend to fall into self-referential inconsistency. They are unable to account adequately for themselves without also risking internal violence. In other words, they must continue to project religious intentions onto prior discourses, including culture itself, in order to assert their own secular legitimacy. Blumenberg argues that the conflicts between contemporary critical theorists and traditional sources of Western culture are inevitable. The conflicts occur where critical theory is construed as an *expropriation* (usurpation) of traditional ideas into the critic's own self-understanding and where critical theorists see their own legitimacy in the *explosion* (negation) of traditional sources of culture.

But Blumenberg also warns that when critical theorists see themselves in such polemically exclusionary ways, then their legitimacy as critics must depend on justifying themselves as something other than the mirror of traditional sources without—at the same time—also falling into self-referential inconsistency.

Habermas also argues similarly when he sees so-called postmodern criticism posturing in antimodern rhetoric (1981, 3–4). In 1980 and 1981, Habermas gave his "Modernity versus Postmodernity" lecture in the city of Frankfurt (on the occasion of his receiving the Theodore W. Adorno prize) and at the New York Institute for the Humanities at New York University, thereby initiating a debate that would preoccupy his scholarship for almost a decade. He opened the lecture by citing a critic in a German newspaper who said, "It is a diagnosis of our times: 'Postmodernity definitely presents itself as Antimodernity.'" Habermas continues, "this statement describes an emotional current of our times which has penetrated all spheres of intellectual life" (3). At the same time, Habermas focused upon the philosophical critics of modernity. He insisted that they have failed to negate modernity, but have perpetuated modernity's splintering into so many instances of individualism. He argued that "instead of giving up on modernity and its project as a lost cause, we should learn from the mistake of those extravagant programs which have tried to negate modernity" (3).

Abounding in the thicket of technical concepts that structures *The Philosophical Discourse on Modernity* (1987), Habermas provides both an apology for "the unfinished project of modernity" and a challenge to those who abandon its rationality. A central premise of the argument is that "postmodernity" (a term Habermas almost always encases in quotation marks) deludes itself when it holds that it has effectively negated modernity's rationality. In its preoccupation with the philosophy of the subject, postmodernity continues the dialectic of the Enlightenment under various and often conflicting images of individuated subjectivity. While I have doubts about the history of negation that Habermas sees abounding in the philosophical discourse of modernity, his judgment nevertheless remains persuasive: where so-called postmodern critics understand themselves in terms of radical oppositional rhetoric, they risk self-referential inconsistency.

Later in this book (chapter 3), I shall argue that where the black theology project hermeneutically follows a polemically exclusionary account of theological reasoning that isolate the project from European theologians, it also puts itself at risk of self-referential inconsistency. It risks internal contradiction as long as it sees itself radically opposed to European religious thought while, at the same time, it remains bound to traditional religious sources retrieved from the European biblical and theological manuscript traditions. Notwithstanding the recent turn among African American theologians to Afrocentric idealism, even these theologians betray an inescapable debt to European nationalist impulses that were apologetically taken up into the black nationalist movements of the late 1960s.

The religious criticism that I propose tries to escape the trap of self-referential contradiction that radical oppositional forms of cultural criticism tend to commit. Religious criticism cannot be successful if it internally regards itself as radically oppositional to—rather than expressive of—the linguistic openings in the critic's own culture. For the religious critic's explanatory and normative judgments about culture are themselves cultured. Therefore, religious criticism shares much with secular criticism insofar as it is rigorously iconoclastic, robbing every mode of discourse, including its own, of achieving any essentialized totality.

Professor William D. Hart of Duke University definitively shows that the primary motive of religious criticism is its unrelentless opposition to every form of cultural idolatry (Hart, 1994). Therefore, religious criticism is not oppositional to secular criticism. Religious criticism seeks to fulfill its iconoclastic functions by exposing the demonic present even in those forms of criticism that parade as liberating and revolutionary projects. It is suspicious of both cultural heroism and cultural idolatry.

Religious criticism is a form of cultural criticism and therefore a culturally descriptive and constructive activity. It attempts to disclose those emancipatory aspects of individuality that each person has a legitimate right to expect of cultural fulfillment within Western democratic societies. As a viable mode of cultural criticism, religious criticism can be enlightening and iconoclastic when it exposes and rejects totalities (race, class, gender, and sexuality) that would deny the cultural fulfillment of persons on the grounds of their differences—whether ethnicity, social status, biological determinants, or sexual orientation. Religious criticism as cultural criticism can be emancipatory and utopian when it sees beyond the debilitating and oppressive structures of culture possibilities for human flourishing and cultural fulfillment. Howard Thurman and Cornel West are two African Americans whose critiques of American racialized culture display the dual intentions (iconoclastic rigor and utopian hope) of religious criticism.

RELIGIOUS CRITICISM IN A RACIALIZED CULTURE

The critique of racial discourse that I propose is not original in African American religious thought. Traces of my project are seen among other African American religious thinkers whose critiques of culture are derived from the interstices of Western philosophy and religion. Two such critics are Howard Thurman and Cornel West. Notwithstanding my differences with Thurman's philosophy of religion and his claims for the viability of a theology of world reconciliation, Thurman remains an effective source of African American religious criticism. And notwithstanding the deeply entrenched Christocentric categories, which tend to define West's account of religious criticism, his idea of prophetic pragmatism remains vital for understanding the religious criticism that I, as a theocentric moralist, propose.

The religious criticism of Thurman is both iconoclastic and utopian. Admittedly the utopian element tends to overshadow the iconoclastic in his writings. Nevertheless, in no text more than in his *The Search for Common Ground* (1986) has the dual religious disposition been so explicated. Several passages by Thurman are worth quoting at length:

> The paradox of conscious life is the ultimate issue here. On the one hand is the absolute necessity for the declaration that states unequivocally the uniqueness of the private life, the awful sense of being an isolate, independent and alone, the great urgency to savor one's personal flavor—to stand over against all the rest of life in contained affirmation. While on the other hand is the necessity to feel oneself as a primary part of all of life, sharing at every level of awareness a dependence upon the same elements in nature, caught up in the ceaseless rhythm of living and dying, with no final immunity against a common fate that finds and holds all living things.
>
> In a sense, therefore, I have been writing this book all my life. Over and over again I have asked myself: What is the common ground that floats the private adventure of the individual or solitary life? Is it merely conceptual, is it only the great idea, the hunger of the heart rationalized into a transcendent God-idea, concept, or notion? Or are these but the scent of the eternal in all living things, perhaps reaching its apotheosis in man, and in the religious man in particular?
>
> Such questions become a personal crisis for a black man living in American Society in the last decades of the twentieth century. (1986, xiv)

Thurman's query remains a telling provocation for African American religious criticism in the last decade of the twentieth century. In turning to Thurman, I am not suggesting that the *common ground* he postulates in his conception of *the Beloved Community* is exactly compatible with the claims that I make for cultural fulfillment. But the parallels are striking. Thurman's philosophy exhibits pragmatic sensibilities grounded on his evolutionary theory of consciousness. He regards human consciousness as essentially a motive and a product of community. And there is a religious pragmatism operative in his estimate of human life and actions. The following quote reveals Thurman's pragmatism:

> Man's experience of his creaturehood suggests that man is in a very real sense one of the products of time-bound evolutionary processes exhibiting characteristics that we associate with the activity of mind: direction and purpose. The very existence of mind in man may be but an expression of man's total response to the history of his organism. But once the existence of mind became possible and therefore a part of the reality of man's experience of the world and of himself, the way was open for him to do directly and deliberately and purposefully what nature has done through eons of time and with much trial and error. (41)

For Thurman, the ground motive that drives human action and thought is community. To be sure, community is a utopian concept. But Thurman also regards the concept as an authentically human possibility because it is thinkable. That is, Thurman is a conceptual realist who regards our highly valued concepts such as love, community, and wholeness as not metaphorical or fictive; but they are human actions. Our moral concepts correspond to something in the world. While community is conceptually ideal, it is nevertheless a human action that is posited in a human form of life:

> Utopia's most pronounced characteristic is a limited and contained community in which the potential of the individ-

ual as well as that of the society can be actualized. Every element is defined in a manner that makes its presence identical with its function. In other words, Utopias are custom made, even though men must live in them. It is as if an entire society and physical environment were fashioned to order . . . . Community as it is experienced in the far-flung hopes of men in all ages finds its greatest fulfillment in a picture of what the collective life of man would be like if it functioned in keeping with man's High destiny. (42–43)

From the passages quoted thus far, the accent falls on Thurman's utopian disposition. Yet it is not altogether clear just how Thurman's thoughts are applicable to the religious critique of culture. It is primarily in the reality of racism that Thurman makes the connection. According to Thurman, racism (whether white or black) undermines our possibilities for actualizing community or bringing about the fulfillment that African Americans rightfully expect by virtue of their citizenship within the United States. In an important passage, Thurman writes:

It becomes clear that if there are any citizens within the state who by definition, stated or implied, are denied freedom of access to the resources of community as established within the state, such persons are assailed at the very foundation of their sense of belonging. . . . This means that such persons are "outsiders" living in the midst of "insiders," required to honor the same demands of sovereignty but denied the basic rewards of sovereignty. This collective or communal denial of the rights and the "rites" of belonging cuts deep into the fabric of the total life of the state. (86–87)

Thurman certainly understood the *insider-outsider* distinction characteristic of the basic dilemma that defines African American cultural life. "Wherever citizens are denied the freedom of access to the resources that make for a sense of belonging, a sense of being totally dealt with, the environment closes in around them, resulting in the schizophrenic dilemma of being inside and outside at one and the same time" (88). Thurman also saw his form of religious criticism representative of the classical race/citizenship dilemma that was crystalized in W. E. B. Du Bois's 1903 classic, *The Souls of Black Folk*. Thurman believed that the dialectic of race and citizenship is not so total as to foreclose on the possibility of internal mediation or transcendence.

For Thurman, the possibility of dialectical mediation or transcendence points to the religious aspects of cultural criticism. This is especially the case when Thurman defines transcendence as not only constitutive of particular being but constitutive of being itself or ultimate reality:

> It is possible for the individual to move out beyond the particular context by which his life is defined and relate to other forms of life from inside their context. This means that there is a boundless realm of which all particular life is but a manifestation. This center is the living thing in man or animal. If a man or an animal can function out of that center, then the boundaries that limit and define can be transcended. (74)

The possibility of transcendence is part and parcel of the epic of African Americans' struggles for freedom in the United States, Thurman insisted. Therefore, he resisted any form of African American criticism that responds to the dialectic of race and citizenship in radically oppositional ways. For Thurman, any form of criticism that cannot admit the possibility of transcendence is not likely to contribute much religiously to social and cultural criticism.

Thurman's notions of transcendence and community are problematic. Their viability for religious criticism is not readily evident; neither can their stability be taken for granted in today's context of criticism. The universe of meaning that circumscribed Thurman's philosophy of religion is now in a crisis of legitimation. Thurman's vision of the continuities, ordering, and cooperative qualities of life, whether in nature or among human beings, as potentiality, is severely mitigated by the unforgiving and often tragic qualities of life. Like Thurman, one may take one's account of community and transcendence from the supposition that they are naturally grounded in the sociobiological conditions of nature and human world consciousness.

However, it is also conceivable that one may equally discover and produce counter-narratives from the same grounds. And these counter-narratives can be as cynical and tragic as Thurman's is an ideally utopian narrative of world reconciliation and reformation of a lost primal community. To be sure, Thurman's philosophy of cultural transcendence and community remained circumscribed by the dual iconoclastic and utopian qualities of religious criticism.

Still, Thurman's thought breeds an optimism about the possibilities of human reconciliation that is hard to sustain in light of our postmodern conditions of cultural fragility, the threat of mass urban and rural nihilism, and the often tragic qualities of daily life. Given our postmodern crises of legitimation, the question of how African American religious criticism can remain a viable source for cultural criticism cannot be ignored. In this regard, Cornel West's idea of prophetic pragmatism is worthy of a close examination.

Recent African American cultural criticism proposes new aesthetic sensibilities, which display the emancipatory and enlightening intentions of African American expressive culture. These sensibilities contribute to a new cultural politics of difference. West has been most engaged in working out the dynamics and intentions of this new cultural politics. For West, the turn to a new cultural aesthetic may also signal the possibility of our redefining African American religious discourse in ways that can support the new cultural politics of difference. West writes:

> To put it bluntly, the new cultural politics of difference consists of creative responses to the precise circumstances of

our present moment—especially those of marginalized First World agents who shun degraded self-representations, articulating instead their sense of the flow of history in light of the contemporary terrors, anxieties and fears of highly commercialized North Atlantic capitalist cultures (with their escalating xenophobia against people of color, Jews, women, gays, lesbians and the elderly). (1993, 3–4)

West describes his own contribution to African American religious criticism as *prophetic pragmatism.* He identifies with the disposition of so-called neopragmatists who exhibit a "widespread disenchantment with the traditional image of philosophy as a transcendental mode of inquiry" and with the aporias of analytic philosophy (1989, 3). West's pragmatism emphasizes "a form of cultural criticism in which the meaning of America is put forward by intellectuals in response to distinct social and cultural crises" (5).

Pragmatism signals a mode of cultural interpretation that aims to be both enlightening and emancipatory. In this regard, pragmatism is not at odds with cultural criticism. In its enlightening intentions, it is a mode of interpretation that explicates the ground motives that drive our social practices. And in its emancipatory intentions, it enables genuine practices that "inspire and instruct contemporary efforts to remake and reform American society and culture" (7). West recognizes that religious beliefs and practices influence contemporary American social practices. Prophetic pragmatism critically makes use of religious beliefs and practices insofar as they constitute the organic circumstances that center the critic's angle of vision. Prophetic pragmatists judge the value of religious beliefs and practices fundamentally by their moral effectiveness in supporting Western democratic humanism and effecting existential hope against those conditions that threaten cultural fulfillment. Such a pragmatism must be iconoclastic insofar as it brings "urgent and compassionate critique to bear on the evils of their day" (233).

In comparison to Thurman's religious criticism, which tends to accent the utopian sensibilities in religious criticism, West highlights the "complex relations [obtaining] between tragedy and revolution, tradition and progress" (226–27). Recognizing that persons have capacities to reshape their social worlds in ways that will advance human flourishing, West stresses the inevitability of the "tragic character of life and history" (228). He explains:

> This sense of the tragic highlights the irreducible predicament of unique individuals who undergo dread, despair, disillusionment, disease, and death and the institutional forms of oppression that dehumanize people. Tragic thought is not confined solely to the plight of the individual; it also applies to social experiences of resistance, revolution, and social reconstruction. Prophetic pragmatism is a form of tragic thought in that it confronts candidly individual and collective experiences of evil in individuals and institutions—with little expectation of ridding the world of all evil. (228)

Prophetic pragmatism does not signal an uncritical optimism about human powers to eradicate evil; neither does it regard the tragic sense of life as if it were total. "Yet it is a kind of romanticism," says West, "in that it holds many experiences of evil to be neither inevitable nor necessary but rather the results of human agency, i.e., choices and actions" (228).

Prophetic pragmatism is bound by two basic dispositions. It is Augustinian insofar as it regards the actualization of humanly intended *paradise* and *utopian perfectionism* to be fated by the inevitability of human finitude; and it is Promethean in its moral optimism about the powers of persons to effect real changes in human societies. It expects that human efforts will be met with some measure of success and new possibilities (229). "In this sense, the praxis of prophetic pragmatism is tragic action with revolutionary intent, usually reformist consequences, and always visionary outlook" (229).

Prophetic pragmatism is oppositional in its critique of those American cultural practices that foreclose on the advancement of genuine democratic goals. However, it is progressive in its support for individuality and democracy. Prophetic pragmatism is a function of cultural criticism:

> The distinctive hallmarks of a prophetic pragmatist are a universal consciousness that promotes an all-embracing democratic and libertarian moral vision, a historical consciousness that acknowledges human finitude and conditionedness, and a critical consciousness which encourages relentless critique and self-criticism for the aims of social change and personal humility. (232)

There is no necessary relation between prophetic pragmatism and professional theology. According to West, "it neither requires a religious foundation nor entails a religious perspective, yet prophetic pragmatism is compatible with certain religious outlooks" (233). But this relation between prophetic pragmatism and religion and theology is organic. In other words, a part of what makes West a pragmatist is the way that his moral sensibilities are informed by religious sensibilities. Thus his religious faith explains something of why he is also a prophetic pragmatist. From West's point of view, there is nothing in the political aims of pragmatism that requires a categorical rejection of religious faith and particularly of Christian faith. And West finds his religious beliefs (at least those that are compatible with "the precious ideals of individuality and democracy") an enabling force in his turn to pragmatism (West, 1989, 235).

Religious faith provides pragmatists who are not exempt from the existential crises that characterize our postmodern conditions with the possibility of an *enabling tradition*, a tradition that can effectively sustain them against the assaults of deep emptiness and pervasive meaninglessness. Having such a religious understanding and appreciation, however, does not require that the prophetic pragmatist become a theologian or be religious in order to understand the plight of the culturally disinherited. Neither does it require that the pragmatist assent uncritically to the narratives of religious groups and the often oppressive ways that these narratives might deny individuality and democracy (233). Rather, "if one is religious, one has wider access into [the] life-worlds" of the oppressed, and "to be religious permits one to devote one's life to accenting the prophetic and progressive potential within those traditions that shape the everyday practices and deeply held perspectives of most oppressed peoples," says West (234).

West's talk about religious faith does not suggest that such a faith is contingent upon theology, because West sees a close identification of theology with the fate of metaphysical philosophy. For West, pragmatism suggests an end to "the Age of Metaphysics." Metaphysics signals a grand objective structure of meaning that anticipates human subjectivity (1988, 267). However, one consequence of pragmatism that West sees in the explosion of metaphysical philosophy is that those disciplines—like metaphysics and theology—that were once charged with the creation of religiously enabling narratives are now caught in the impasses of a postmodern crisis. West writes:

> We are witnessing an increasing incredulity toward master- or meta-narratives, be they Christian, Marxist, or liberal. We live in a time of cultural disarray and social decay, an age filled with ruins and fragments. Hence, our intellectual landscapes are littered with allegorical tales of deterioration rather than dramatic narratives of reconciliation. (1988, 270)

West is confident that Christian narratives can continue to enlighten persons about the consequences of human finitude and enable them to actualize instances of genuine democratic practices. Nevertheless, he admits that "even legitimate narrative modes may have highly limited potency and pertinence in a world in which any sense of the whole has been lost." In such a world, even prophetic pragmatism might well be seen as just so many "vestigial clingings to long lost ways, the planting of one's feet on a world that is gone" (270).

Prophetic pragmatism does not only achieve specificity as religious criticism by offering theological descriptions and categories that elucidate both the social evils and the ways African Americans have traditionally given meaning to their struggles and their capacities to survive and remain human. But as religious criticism, prophetic pragmatism "always keeps open a skeptical eye to avoid dogmatic traps, premature closures, formulaic formulations or rigid conclusions" (1993, 23). Prophetic pragmatism is rigorously iconoclastic in its attempt to track the ways that cultural activities threaten individuality, novelty, and moral agency (23).

The corollary to this iconoclastic intention is a creative, transformative praxis that seeks "new kinds of connections, affinities and communities across empire, nation, region, race, gender and sexual orientation" (29). For West, difference constitutes a good that centers the transcendent possibilities of democracy. Like Thurman before him, West proposes a form of cultural criticism that is both iconoclastic and utopian. For both critics, the stereoscopic gaze constitutes the normative focus of African American religious criticism.

Both Thurman and West exhibit aspects of the religious criticism that I advance. Both thinkers are African Americans who take their point of departure in the critique of culture from African American life in the United States. While consciously aware of the pervasive existential influences of white racism on black life, neither thinker regards racist influences as so pervasive as to render black life totalized by its demonic consequences. To be sure, their discourses are dialectically structured. However, neither thinker regards the dialectics of race (race and freedom, insider and outsider, group and personality) as having either an absolutely negative function—such that one pole is canceled by the other—or an absolutely positive representational function—such that the one pole is necessarily justified in terms of the other.

Both Thurman and West hold open the possibility that the apparently binary oppositions that characterize racial discourse can be transcended. But transcendence requires a cause or loyalty that is sufficiently categorical to include within itself both the cultural aspects of group life and personality. For Thurman, the dialectics of race is transcended in the idea of the beloved community. For West, radical democracy serves the function of transcendence. I call the elements of transcendence that these thinkers commend *cultural fulfillment*.

▪ ▪ ▪

I have tried to develop a general theory of cultural fulfillment that is substantive enough to center the dual dimensions of cultural and religious criticism. Cultural fulfillment is the reflexive integration of basic human needs and subjective goods. It involves the satisfaction of categorical goods that human beings minimally require for maintaining biological life (life, safety, work, leisure, knowledge, and the like). It also involves the satisfaction of subjective goods (friendship, peace of mind, integrity of conscience, and spiritual meaning) that individuals require for alleviating subjective alienation, assuring subjective equilibrium, and realizing positive personalities. Fulfillment of such needs and goods motivates the cultural activities of persons within society.

When cultural fulfillment is substantively explicated, it is difficult to confine cultural analysis to conceptual dichotomies or binary oppositions such as the real and ephemeral, phenomena and epiphenomena, subjective and material, and the community and individual. In cultural criticism, it is neither the goods and ends of the group alone, nor those of the individual alone, that bind the loyalties of the critic.

Critics need to be aware of the vicious consequences that follow from cultic devotion to both the group and the individual. Such an awareness is displayed in the religious criticism of both Thurman and West. When the religious critic exposes the demonic aspects of both communalism and individualism, the critic carries out an iconoclastic function in cultural criticism. Thurman and West advance the necessity of iconoclastic rigor in African American cultural criticism. They also correlate this iconoclastic function with utopian prospects for cultural fulfillment in their respective languages of the beloved community and radical democracy. In African American religious criticism, such languages signify possibilities for cultural transcendence from the debilitating and oppressive structures of North American racialized culture.

Chapters 2–3 extend the dual elements of African American cultural and religious criticism to the critique of categorical racism and racial apologetics in African American cultural philosophy and ontological blackness in African American theology.

two

CATEGORICAL RACISM
AND RACIAL APOLOGETICS

■ ■ ■

No adequate critique of racial discourse can proceed without paying attention to the ways that race linguistically develops in multiple contexts and with a variety of appropriations in Western culture. In this chapter, the concept of ontological blackness is situated within the philosophical discourse of modern racism. Other critics—such as Richard Popkins (1977–78), Cornel West (1982), and David Theo Goldberg (1993)—have done more extensive genealogies of modern racism. However, this chapter is a brief genealogy of the impact of racial discourse in African American cultural philosophy. This chapter is framed by several critical themes: categorical racism, white racial ideology, and racial apologetics.

Categorical racism appropriates a species logic in which every individual member of a species shares essential traits that identify the member within the species. No accidental or particular instances of individuation (historical, economic, manners, or customs) can disconnect the individual member from the species for the individual necessarily or categorically belongs in the species if it shares all the essential traits identifying the species. Two tasks of Enlightenment and Romantic cultural philosophy (18th to early 19th-century north European philosophy in Scotland, France, and Germany) were to isolate and describe those essential features that differentiate the European consciousness from others.

European philosophers developed a philosophy of difference in terms of rationality, aesthetics, morals, and race. In their discourse, racial consciousness became a defining category in the politics of European difference. European intellectuals sought to disclose European genius as an explanatory category for the progressive, historical movement of the modern age. Categorical racism allowed these intellectuals to legitimize the modern age in terms of comparative cultural anthropology.

In this chapter, I trace the development of categorical racism in two representative figures, Immanuel Kant (1724–1804) and Thomas Jefferson (1743–1826). I highlight how their comparative critiques of European and African aesthetic consciousness were conducted under the umbrella of categorical racism and white racial ideology. White racial ideology has had at least three functions: (1) it justified the supremacy of European consciousness on a comparative and hence a scientific basis; (2) it provided historical and moral rationalizations for the spread of European imperialism throughout the world; and (3) it justified the exclusion of blacks and other colonized peoples from civic republican citizenship.

Categorical racism and white racial ideology occasioned the preoccupation of African American cultural philosophy with racial apologetics. In their attempts to reassure the dignity, respect, and humanity of African peoples, African American cultural philosophers put forward a counter-discourse to white racial ideology. Their discourse exhibits common features: (1) it rejected categorical racism and white racial ideology's negative projections of blacks; (2) it explained historically—not categorically—the moral failures associated with blacks; (3) it positively regarded blacks' racial identity as commensurable with civic republican humanism; and (4) it advanced the groups' racial uplift as expressive of black cultural genius and civilization. If categorical racism justified white racial ideology, then black racial apologetics justified ontological blackness in African American cultural philosophy.

AESTHETICS AND WHITE RACIAL IDEOLOGY

The relation between white racial ideology and black apologetics is circular. Each rises out of modern racial aesthetics. The aesthetic theory of the European Enlightenment and the Romantic period, from David Hume (1711–1776), Immanuel Kant (1724–1804), Johann Herder (1744–1803), Friedrich Schiller (1759–1805), Johann Gottlieb Fichte (1762–1814), to G. W. F. Hegel (1770–1831), was preoccupied with establishing neither the rules nor the repetition of ancient form. Nor was it fundamentally concerned with the refinement of taste. Rather, in a turn toward history and culture, Enlightenment and Romantic aesthetic theory tended to differentiate itself against taste (Tonelli, 1973, 293–97; Wittkower, 1973, 297–312). Occasioned as it was by the revival of classical humanism in European philosophy, aesthetic theory appropriated classical models for historical purposes. The spirit of the ancients, which was solidified in an imperialist culture and morality, was now reinscribed in the nationalist impulses of the modern nation–states of Europe. Aesthetic theory was in the service of a cultural philosophy of Europe.

Enlightenment and Romantic aesthetic theory turned on the problem of relating experience and taste with historical and natural boundaries. The relation was mediated in a symbolic, expressive play of freedom, which was itself identified as a European cultural motive. The unity of experience and taste with history and culture was resolved in a cultural philosophy of European genius. Just as cultural advancement in the classical age of Greek and Roman antiquities owed much to the success of political virtue and wisdom over the natural forces of fate and fortune, so the age of Europe was emerging on an epochal threshold in which critical philosophy would break the impasses of nature's determinative transactions as well as conventions of history and tradition.

The cultural philosophy of Europe was determined by the cult of genius over taste. As I show in chapter 4, genius is not only a quality of individual personality. It is also representational of the cultural constellations that preside over the birth and fortune of a nation or people. The burden of genius is visible in the ways that art and music, literature and drama, science and politics, and religion and philosophy are all recognized as symbolic representations of exceptional, categorical traits of European people.

When Kant compared the genius of European peoples to African peoples in terms of a fundamental distinction between the sublime and the beautiful and mere taste, he solidified the terms in which symbolic, expressive aesthetics would be apologetically taken up into the cultural philosophy of African Americans. In *Observations on the Feeling of the Beautiful and Sublime,* written in 1763, Kant writes:

> The Negroes of Africa have by nature no feeling that rises above the trifling. Mr. Hume challenges anyone to cite a single example in which a Negro has shown talents, and asserts that among the hundreds of thousands of blacks who are transported elsewhere from their countries, although many of them have even been set free, still not a single one was ever found who presented anything great in art or science or any other praiseworthy quality, even though among the whites some continually rise aloft from the lowest rabble, and through superior gifts earn respect in the world. So fundamental is the difference between these two races of man, and it appears to be as great in regard to mental capacities as in color. The religion of fetishes so wide spread among them is perhaps a sort of idolatry that sinks as deeply into the trifling as appears to be possible to human nature. A bird feather, a cow's horn, a conch shell, or any other common object, as soon as it becomes consecrated by a few

words, is an object of veneration and invocation in swearing oaths. The Blacks are very vain but in the Negro's way, and so talkative that they must be driven apart from each other with thrashing. (1960, 110–11)

Kant's racial aesthetic judgments have had an effective career in the subsequent cultural philosophy of European genius. In terms of its content and supporting arguments, Kant's categorical judgments are comparable to David Hume's antecedent British argument (West, 1982, 47–65; Popkins, 1977–78, 210–25; Goldberg, 1992, 31ff.). On the American scene, the European pejorative critiques of African aesthetic consciousness are categorically inscribed in Thomas Jefferson's portrayal of African slaves and free blacks in his 1787 English publication of *Notes on the State of Virginia* (1970, 14–21).

Jefferson provides a defense for returning free blacks and mulattoes to Africa. He argues that any proposal that seeks to retain and incorporate "the blacks into the state and thus save the expense of supplying by importation of white settlers, the vacancies they will leave" fails to recognize that there are fundamental differences between blacks and whites, which make such a plan politically and morally vicious. Jefferson argues that these differences ought not to be thought of as differences of accidents, the cultivation of manners, or the circumstances of birth, which as we shall see shortly is the Lockean basis for political inequality. For Jefferson, these differences are natural, organic, and categorically applied to the race. These categorical distinctions might easily be classified as aesthetic, physical, psychological, cultural, and historical. Race was the organizing category.

Aesthetically, Jefferson argues, the "eternal monotony" of that "immovable veil of black which covers the emotions of the other race" is less preferable in beauty to the "fine mixture of red and white, the expression of every passion by greater or less suffusions of color in the one." And the preference among blacks for the "flowing hair" and "more elegant symmetry of form" of the white woman or of the "Orangutan" to that of the black woman speaks to the superiority of white over black. Physically, blacks are anatomically different from whites. These anatomical differences of the endocrine system, for instance, are what account for their having "a very strong and disagreeable odor" and for their being more tolerant of heat than cold. They require less sleep and are prone to staying up at all hours of the night at the impetus of "the slightest amusement," despite the fact that they must be at work around dawn. In valor and sexuality, blacks are moved more by instinct of nature than by "coolness or steadiness" or by a "tender delicate mixture of sentiment and sensation." They are abnormal in natural sentiment and feeling, transient in grief, and passive in affliction.

Psychologically, the memories of blacks are as good as whites, but their reason is inferior and their imaginations dull, tasteless, and anomalous (not worth mentioning). Jefferson suggests that these traits of mind appear to be basic and not circumstantial.

Rationally, blacks are not able to understand Euclidian geometry or "utter a thought above the level of plain narration." They do not show any "elementary trait of painting or sculpture." Culturally, they seem more gifted in music than whites, especially with regard to tune and time, but "whether they will be equal to the composition of a more extensive run of melody, or of complicated harmony is yet to be proved." And "if misery is the parent of poetry" Jefferson said, and "God has surely given them over to misery enough, yet they have no genius for poetry." Their few poets are not worth critical attention. And historically, when compared with the slaves of Greece or Rome, they show no genius as did "Epictetus, Terence, and Phaedrus" who were all "of the race of whites." Jefferson therefore concludes that it is not circumstances that vitiate the cultural genius of blacks. It is "this unfortunate difference of color, and perhaps of faculty, [that] is a powerful obstacle to the emancipation of these people." And even if emancipated, these distinctions are enough to warrant that blacks be "removed beyond the reach of mixture" in order that their blood should not taint the white race in America.

Behind Kant's and Jefferson's critiques of the African aesthetic consciousness lies a distinct metaphysical structure that is based on categorical racism and underlies a white racial ideology. White racial ideology, in the West, was dependent on the advancement of a species logic derived from the natural law tradition. The negative corollary of the natural law species logic is the projection of a pseudospecies in which people of African descent are regarded as belonging to a separate species. In intelligence, understanding, and cultural practices, African peoples are said, categorically, to exhibit no spark of cultural genius. White racial ideology structured the liberal politics of democratic exclusion in North America. And such a politic owed much to John Locke's theory of natural inequality. In white racial ideology, blackness became a fundamental category of natural inequality.

Uday S. Mehta and Barbara J. Fields explain the relation between political exclusion, natural inequality, and white racial ideology. Mehta is deeply invested in the political philosophy of British thinkers John Locke and John S. Mill. Discussing the seventeenth century philosopher John Locke (1632–1704), Mehta sees the interplay of natural law metaphysics and historical existence providing theoretical conditions for the Lockean doctrine of natural inequality and liberal exclusionary politics. It would be Locke's theory of natural inequality that justified the exclusion of blacks from participation in civic republican citizenship. Mehta asks how it is conceivable that "liberal principles with their attending universal constituency get undermined in such a manner as to politically disenfranchise various people" (1990, 428). Two answers characterize the British argument: natural inequality and social conventions.

The rationality of liberal democratic exclusion involves a circularity of reasoning whereby those who are politically excluded are said to "manifest certain political incompetencies" that are then "justified by a plethora of anthropological descriptions that serve to buttress the claim of incompetence" (428). Under such a logic, one only has to establish a set of criteria (Y, Y1, Y2, Yn) which X formally is supposed to meet in order to properly (categorically) belong to a political community. Then define X in such a way that X is unable to meet certain conditions (Y1 and Y2) among the criteria of permissibility. At those points where X does not meet Y, it is necessarily excluded from the community. In this way, at least theoretically, there exists no inconsistency between the rhetoric of political inclusion, on the one hand, and the fact that some are naturally excluded, on the other.

However, the central argument that justifies the politics of racial exclusion is based on the role that social conventions play in Locke's philosophical anthropology. The principal sources of Lockean political exclusionary practices are not in human nature (formal criteria) but in the circumstances of birth (material criteria). Mehta's position is that Locke's exclusionary rhetoric is legitimized "on a complex constellation of social structures and social conventions to delimit, stabilize, and legitimize without explicitly restricting the universal referent of his foundational commitments" (435). The problematic space between liberal theory and practice is best construed as obtaining within a whole range of circumstances in which persons are embedded—circumstances that are deep, thick, inscrutable, and simply in the background of any construction of philosophical and political rhetoric.

This means that the conditions undermining the inclusionary intentions of democratic citizenship (conditions based on natural human rights) are prior to the construction of self-evidential truths and the theoretical delineation of political right:

> Terms such as "English gentry," "breeding," "gentleman," "honor," "discretion," "inheritance," and "servant" derive their meaning and significance from a specific set of cultural norms. They refer to a constellation of social practices riddled with a hierarchial and exclusionary density. They draw

on and encourage conceptions of human beings that are far from abstract and universal and in which the anthropological minimum is buried under a thick set of social inscriptions and signals. They chart a terrain full of social credentials. It is a terrain that the natural individual equipped with universal capacities must negotiate before these capacities assume the form necessary for political inclusion. In this, they circumscribe and order the particular form that the universalistic foundations of Lockean liberalism assume. It is a form that can and historically has left an exclusionary imprint in the concrete instantiation of liberal practices. (438–39)

Particularly striking in Mehta's account of the Lockean theory of political inequality is the peculiar liberal silence about race as a circumstance that mitigates universal right. One factor may explain this silence. While the languages of natural right and convention, manners, circumstances, and property achieved a regulative status in the development of Lockean liberal politics, race had not yet been invented or discovered as an exclusionary category in liberal politics. Categorical racism had not achieved the ideological stability that it would have in eighteenth century America, after the American revolution and in Jefferson's subsequent oration (Fields, 1990, 95–118).

Barbara Fields, an African American social critic, argues that race ideology grew up out of concrete historical conditions and interests. Race was added to an already existing constellation of exclusionary circumstances that effectively excluded English indentured servants, women, and children, says Fields. Therefore, it was added to exclusionary practices already rooted in custom and law, and convention and manners. Race also made a convenient justification for the perpetual enslavement of some human beings where British law prohibited such a practice toward the English. This justification gave protection to large landowners, ensuring for them a stable, inexpensive capital that would guard them against violent resistance by "armed Englishmen resentful at being denied the rights of Englishmen and disposing of the material and political resources to make their resentment felt" (105).

Race provided a linguistic category that effectively answered the inconsistencies of a political ideology that metaphysically shaped freedom under natural human right (inclusion) but also had to account for political exclusionary practices. According to Fields:

> Race explained why some people could rightly be denied what others took for granted: namely, liberty, supposedly a self-evident gift of nature's God. But there was nothing to explain until most people could, in fact, take liberty for granted—as the indentured servants and disenfranchised freedmen of colonial America could not. Nor was there anything calling for a radical explanation where everyone in society stood in a relation of inherited subordination to someone else: servant to master, serf to nobleman, vassal to overlord, overlord to king, king to the King of Kings and Lord of Lords. (114)

With the progressive democratization of the American colonies, culminating in the American revolution, natural inequality justified the endemic inconsistencies between the inclusionary intentions of American democracy and the exclusionary intentions of white racial ideology. In her own critical account of American citizenship, Judith N. Shklar persuasively summarizes the point when she writes:

> What renders any group or individual unfit for citizenship is economic dependence, race, and gender, which are all socially created or hereditary conditions. Such rules would seem to imply a political system that is in no sense democratic or liberal, but it was never that simple, because Americans have lived with extreme contradictions for most of their

history by being dedicated to political equality as well as to its complete rejection. (1991, 8)

To sum up, categorical racism and white racial ideology justified the racial consciousness of the modern age by providing rhetorical conditions for positively differentiating the European cultural genius from others. European genius sees among the particular motives of ancient and traditional societies universal motives. These universal motives are represented in the cultural activities of philosophy, science, aesthetics, and cultural studies. In this conception of difference, every particular difference is culturally significant insofar as it is taken up into the self-understanding of European cultural genius.

Notwithstanding the possibility of universality in cultural development, when race was added to other natural inequalities (age, family, caste, and the like), the Lockean doctrine of natural inequality provided a rational category by which to justify the categorical exclusion of blacks from democratic citizenship. The apologetic task of African American cultural philosophers was to construct a counter-discourse to categorical racism and white racial ideology. Racial apologetics would be in the service of an African American philosophy of black culture.

RACIAL APOLOGETICS

African American cultural philosophy defined itself historically in relation to theories of African aesthetic consciousness inherited from the European Enlightenment and Romantic cultural philosophy. The black aesthetic must be seen in dialectical relation to white racial ideology. The cultural philosophies of African Americans from the early nineteenth century to the late twentieth century would justify themselves in terms of both influences, and hence in terms of a blackness that whiteness created. African American critics have tended to define themselves by the metaphysical determinants of white racial ideology. In the tradition of African American cultural philosophy, African American cultural activities achieve legitimacy as they reflect the cultural genius of the people. Disclosing this genius is both the motive and the end of black subjectivity.

Yet black subjectivity is subjugated under the totality of racial ideology in a double sense. Negatively, it is answerable to the exclusionary practices of white racism. Positively, racial ideology sets the terms of classical African American cultural philosophy, from David Walker's *Appeal* (1828), to Booker T. Washington (1856–1915), W. E. B. DuBois (1868–1963), Marcus Garvey (1887–1940), Howard Thurman (1900–1981), Dr. Martin Luther King, Jr. (1929–1968), and the recent debates occurring among contemporary black intellectuals about the relevance of the Du Boisean double-consciousness to the new cultural politics of difference (Gerald Early, 1993).

David Walker's *Appeal* (original, 1828; reprinted, 1970, 57–105) must be seen as a counter-discourse on the cultural aesthetic of thinkers like Hume and Kant, and in particular Jefferson. Walker's *Appeal* is an artistic production that attempts to appropriate the style of neoclassical rhetoric among the enlightened classes of the nineteenth century. Walker's style is expressive of the influences of classical rhetoric on the nineteenth century American intellectual. After all, it is this class that Walker hoped to morally persuade against Jefferson's stinging criticism that blacks manifest a natural inferiority in their inability to move beyond narrative to argument. Walker's rhetoric counter-factually challenges Jefferson's assumptions.

Walker takes issue with Jefferson's claims that the failure of moral manliness and cultural genius among African Americans is a matter of nature and not of circumstances. He takes great pains to show that these failures are not conditions of nature and hence not categorical. Rather, they are consequences of the long era of degradation and wretchedness in which blacks acquired habits that disrupted their capacities to discern what is morally required of them as a people. The principal causes of their moral and cultural failure are servility, ignorance, and oppression. However, the actions of African American slaves and free blacks tend to buttress claims made for the cultural aesthetics of the Enlightenment. And on this point, Walker's oration is eloquent and emotive.

> Oh! colored people of these United States, I ask you, in the name of that God who made us, have we, in consequence of oppression, nearly lost the spirit of man, and in no very trifling degree, adopted that of brutes? Do you answer No?—I ask you, then, what set of men can you point me to, in all the world, who are so abjectly employed by their oppressors, as we are by our *natural enemies*? How can, Oh! how can those enemies but say that we and our children are not of the HUMAN FAMILY, but were made by our creator to be an inheritance to them and theirs forever? How can the slave holders but say that they can bribe the best colored person in the country, to sell his brethren for a trifling sum of money, and take that atrocity to confirm them in their avaricious opinion, that we were made to be slaves to them and their children? (75; Walker's emphasis)

Hume, Kant, and Jefferson argue that the natural dispositions of African slaves are inferior to those of whites. But Walker fears that the servility and ignorance that African slaves tend to exhibit only confirm these Europeans' aesthetic judgments. Answering the charge is not the white man's burden, says Walker. It is the burden of African Americans:

> For my part, I am glad Mr. Jefferson has advanced his positions for your sake; for you will either have to contradict or confirm him by your own actions and not what our friends have said or done for us; for those things are other men's labors and do not satisfy the Americans who are waiting for us to prove to them ourselves, that we are MEN before they will be willing to admit that fact. (76)

Walker represents the interruptions of slavery's brutality in terms of the moral "manliness" of Carthage's Hanibal, the Haitian revolution, and most emphatically in terms of the independence of the black churches under the leadership of Bishop Richard Allen (93). Walker's notion of *moral manliness* is not only a recurring theme in the subsequent history of African American cultural philosophy; it is architectonic.

As Du Bois took up the cultural philosophy advanced by Walker, he circumscribed African American reflections on their cultural practices under a negro/freedom dialectic. Du Bois defined and described the self-understanding of black folk within the dialectics of a double-consciousness or a twoness (1982, 45–46ff.). The word *folk* ought to be understood as analogous to the German *Volkgeist,* meaning the spirit of the people. Hence, it categorically reflects the broad cultural-ethical life of the African American people. Therefore, it refers to the cultural experience that defines black existence within the ethos of American society. Du Bois's classic account of this dialectic describes African Americans as self-consciously aware that they are both Americans and black; hence, the negro/freedom dialectic.

African Americans are aware that their cultural identities emerge from and are linked with American society. They are also aware that they are alienated from that society by the color of their skin, by a color line. African Americans are informed by civic republican ideals that frame the ethical constitution of American society. But they are also aware that they do not participate in or enjoy the benefits of full citizenship in American life and society.

Rhetorically, Du Bois tackled the question of African American exclusion from the benefits of American citizenship in language as provocative as it is haunting:

> Why did God make me an outcast and a stranger in mine own house? . . . After the Egyptian and Indian, the Greek and Roman, the Teuton and Mongolian, the Negro is a sort

of seventh son, born with a veil, and gifted with second-sight in this American world—a world which yields him no true self-consciousness, but only lets him see himself through the revelation of the other world. It is a peculiar sensation, the double-consciousness, the sense of always looking at one's self through the eyes of others, of measuring one's soul by the tape of a world that looks on in amused contempt and pity. One ever feels his twoness—an American, a Negro; two souls, two thoughts, two unreconciled strivings; two warring ideals in one dark body, whose dogged strength alone keeps it from being torn asunder.

The history of the American Negro is the history of this strife—this longing to attain self-conscious manhood, to merge his double self into a better and truer self. . . . This then is the end of his striving; to be a coworker in the kingdom of culture, to escape both death and isolation, to husband and use his best powers and his latent genius. (1982, 45–46)

Du Bois's dialectic has become a stable matrix for reading African American cultural practices throughout the twentieth century. Peter J. Paris argues that this double self-understanding of African Americans is still helpful in the interpretation of African American religious practices. On Paris's account, "this moral conflict permeates all aspects of their common life, that is, their autonomy, moral agency, political orientation, and understanding of power" (1985, xiii).

Paris insists that the dialectic of race and citizenship embraces every aspect of African American socio-cultural identity including African American class consciousness. Therefore, on Paris's account (notwithstanding whatever class differentials might genuinely be recognized to exist among African Americans), the social, cultural, economic, religious, and political formations of their experience are circumscribed by the Du Boisean negro/freedom configuration. At the end of this chapter, the confidence that Paris shows in the Du Boisean dialectic will be tested in light of contemporary critiques of the Du Boisean double-consciousness.

Until recent times, particularly in the political discourse about the black middle class and the problem of the urban underclass, race overshadowed questions of intraracial classism, gender bias, and homophobia. These problems are bracketed or seen as, in some sense, subordinate to the all-pervasive umbrella of racism and the veil of blackness. In the cultural philosophies of Booker T. Washington, W. E. B. Du Bois, and Marcus Garvey, the problem of race (historically identified as "the negro problem") dominated the flow of the questions that guided their critiques of culture. It also shaped their emancipatory visions of black culture. Yet the problem of systematic racial discrimination, legitimized as it was by white racial ideology, worked itself out among these thinkers in rival discourses. Each discourse was aimed at overcoming the alienation and oppression that African Americans experienced after abolition and reconstruction.

The historic debates among African American political leaders, such as Washington, Du Bois, and Garvey, were not about the right of full citizenship for African Americans. These leaders were convinced of the rightness of full citizenship for and the full participation of African American people in American society. Neither were their debates about the republican ideals that shaped the constitution of American society. African American leaders did not debate liberal ideology. Their debates centered around practical questions like how to integrate best, as full citizens, African Americans into the American democratic experiment, or whether integration is a real possibility for African Americans.

Washington's vision for African Americans and their integration in American society crystalized in his classic Atlanta Exposition speech in 1895 (1974, 578–87). In that speech Washington clearly had in mind the recent memory of the Republican reconstruction of the south. The gains and promises of full citizenship had been systematically undermined by the legal legitimation of racial exclusion in the politics of Jim Crow. Washington remained fundamentally committed to nothing short of full citizenship for African Americans. For him, the body politic was compelling and friendship was the proposed means for advancing African American democratic citizenship.

Washington's speech served multiple purposes. It explained the regressive, racial politics after the failure of reconstruction and it served a meliorating role that would satisfy white fears and advance the uplift of the race. Washington argued that the emancipatory intentions in reconstruction failed because they were hostile to the customs and the way of life in the south. Instead of promoting the well being of southern blacks, reconstruction placed them in the precarious position of being perceived as enemies of a southern social world that was ill-prepared for a politicized black citizenry. Therefore, Washington's good neighbor rhetoric advanced the position that the white south must learn to trust the freed blacks, no longer as slaves, but now as faithful loyal friends of and participants in the body politic. And he argued that meliorating the interests of both blacks and whites in the south would be best effected if both races were committed to the south's economic growth. Washington believed that the moral and political education of African Americans will promote the uplift of the race into full citizenship, but the race must first prove itself a friend of the republic. And in the south, that meant carrying one's own weight in the economy. He challenged blacks to:

> Cast down your buckets in agriculture, mechanics, in commerce, in domestic service, and in the professions. And in this connection it is well to bear in mind that whatever other sins the South may be called upon to bear, when it comes to business, pure and simple, it is in the South that the Negro is given a man's chance in the commercial world, and in nothing is this exposition more eloquent than in emphasizing this chance. (584)

The quote accents the interstices of blacks' real interests in the economic life of the South, but it also frames such interests within the boundaries of black masculinity.

To be sure, Washington's personal spirituality played an important role in determining his ethics. His piety was characteristically evangelical and individualistic, emphasizing moral character over rational religion. Washington articulated this spirituality in a passage worth quoting at length:

> I sometimes fear that in our great anxiety to push forward we lay too much stress upon our former condition. We should think less of our former growth and more of the present and of the things which go to retard or hinder that growth. . . . St Paul says: "But the fruit of the spirit is love, joy, peace, longsuffering, gentleness, goodness, faith, meekness, temperance; against such there is no law." I believe that it is possible for a race, as it is for an individual, to learn to live up to such a high atmosphere that there is no human law that can prevail against it. There is no law that can affect the Negro in relation to his singing, his peace, and his self control. Wherever I go I would enter St. Paul's atmosphere and, living through and in that spirit, we will grow and make progress and notwithstanding discouragement and mistakes, we will become an increasingly strong part of the Christian citizenship of this republic. (Washington and Du Bois, 1970, 40–41)

Washington believed that the virtues peculiar to an individual's piety are translatable into a set of political virtues. Such a translation, however, tends to treat racial exclusion as merely a set of attitudes that can be adjusted, rather than treating it as a structural evil. This is not to say that Washington's politics had no mechanism for political transformation; the Tuskegee platform is evidence of such a program. Washington defended a liberal-conservative mode of criticism. But its underlying profession of a body politic, the preparation of a territory for democracy, and the virtues suited to a Christian republican body, all had to be integrated and acquired through universal education in which vocational education occupied top priority. And the advancement of African Americans into full citizenship within American civil society had to be implemented gradually.

Washington's program was well received by the white south. He was perceived to be a friend of the south and its economic life. Even Du Bois, at first, showed enthusiasm for Washington's Atlanta speech. He wrote in a letter to Washington: "Let me congratulate you upon your phenomenal success at Atlanta— it was a word fitly spoken. Sincerely yours, W. E. B. Du Bois" (Washington, *Papers* 4, 1975, 39). However, the speech also contributed to the fragility of black politics in the twentieth century. For while Du Bois initially showed appreciation for Washington's speech, he soon became "the voice of opposition" against Washington's accommodationist politics. In a critique of Washington, Du Bois would later write:

> His programme of industrial education, conciliation of the South, and submission and silence as to civil and political right, was not wholly original; the Free Negroes from the 1830s up to our time had striven to build industrial schools, and the American Missionary Association had from the first taught various trades; and Price and others had sought a way of honorable alliance with the best of the Southerners. But Mr. Washington first indissolubly linked these things; he put enthusiasm, unlimited energy, and perfect faith into his programme, and changed it from a by-path into a veritable Way of Life. (1982, 79–80)

For Du Bois, Washington's liberal-conservative politics was dubbed "the Atlanta compromise" (80). Du Bois went on to say, "Mr. Washington represents in Negro thought the old attitude of adjustment and submission" (87). The Tuskegee platform was criticized for being too strongly accommodating to the economic, commercialistic, and industrialistic trends of the nation:

it was criticized for being a "gospel of Work and Money to such an extent as apparently almost to completely overshadow the higher aim of life," that aim being "manly self-respect" (87). Du Bois was convinced that "manly self-respect is worth more than lands and houses, and that a people who voluntarily surrender such respect, or cease striving for it, are not worth civilizing" (87).

Washington's program was criticized, in the end, for being ideologically bankrupt, politically impotent, and spiritually untenable because it justified the immediate "opportunities at hand" and the flight from the "higher ideals and aspirations" of black masculinity (90). Du Bois articulated a rival cultural philosophy in defense of the inclusion of the African Americans into American civil society. In presenting his rival discourse, Du Bois also retrieved another message from Christianity, the message of absolute justice as it was proclaimed by the classical Hebrew prophets and imitated by David Walker and other public theologians of the nineteenth century.

Like Washington, Du Bois was committed to a body politic. But unlike Washington, he was fully committed to confrontation and agitation as the means toward the full integration of African Americans into American civil society (1972, 55). Demand, persistence, pride, and decent self-respect form the constitutive themes in Du Bois's cultural philosophy (71). In his book *The Souls of Black Folk*, Du Bois attempted to develop a cultural philosophy of black experience that advocates the transformation of the African American creative and intellectual energies from the context of personal development (individual subjectivity) to social power.

Freedom emerges in racial progress and an ethic of black masculinity. Such an ethic is defined in terms of agitation and confrontation. And legitimizing such an ethic is the task of African American cultural philosophy under the ideological guardianship of the black bourgeoisie. African American cultural philosophy requires structural transformations of African American cultural potentialities. Such transformations are directed by African American elites whose activities are themselves guided by social justice and whose creative powers and energies must create racial dissonance within American political culture. By means of confrontation, African Americans must create openings in the republic for the advancement of the people.

Religiously, Du Bois's privileging of black masculinity and his no compromise temperament in politics were informed and controlled rhetorically by the prophetic theme of absolute social justice. This theme legitimized Du Bois's subversive Christianity. He was adamant in his insistence that Washington's politics is not only politically misguided but also religiously effeminate. He argued that both the church and the state in America ought to be controlled no longer by the Jesus who said: "Come on to me all you that labor and I will give you rest; take my yolk upon [yourselves] and learn of me; for I am meek and lowly in heart; and [you] shall find rest for your souls. For my yolk is easy and my burdens are light" (Washington and Du Bois, 1970, 122). Du Bois's Jesus is envisioned as standing in the tradition of the classical prophets and their ethic of absolute social justice.

Du Bois understood the precepts of Jesus to be explicitly concerned with ultimate political equality. And it is this emphasis, Du Bois said, that was propagated in the political theology of Methodists and Baptists, and sustained in the politics and rhetoric of abolition (132). Du Bois saw himself in solidarity with this grand motif. In a very important passage, he writes:

> It may be that the price of the Black man's survival in America and in the modern world, will be a long and shameful night of subjection to caste and segregation. If so, he will pay it, doggedly, silently, unfalteringly, for the sake of human liberty and the souls of his children's children. But as he stoops he will remember the indignation of that Jesus who cried, yonder behind heaving seas and years: "Woe unto you scribes and Pharisees, hypocrites, that strain out a gnat and swallow a camel"—as if God cared a whit whether

His Sons are born of maid, wife or widow so long as His
church sits deaf to His own calling: "Ho! everyone that [is
thirsty], come to the waters and he that [has] no money;
come, buy and eat; [yes], come, buy wine and milk without
money and without price!" (191)

The last biblical reference in the quote is perhaps most revealing of Du Bois's emancipatory intentions. It not only in-
vokes the witness of the prophets, it also constitutes an imitation
of the prophets. Du Bois's retrieval of the prophetic utterance of
Isaiah (Isaiah 55:1) reveals his eschatological hope that absolute
equality will be embodied in concrete human relations. But Du
Bois's imitation of the prophets also reveals an implicit criticism
of the present state of America's market economy.

For Du Bois, a social justice based on absolute, universal
equality and right must be politically, ethically, and theologically
controlling in African American cultural philosophy. Yet many
charged it as placing ideals before *bread and butter*. And in many
ways, it was this aspect of Du Bois's politics that led other African American leaders, at the turn of the century, to find Washington's voice a persuasive alternative.

But with the emergence of Jamaican-born Marcus Garvey,
African American cultural philosophy was transformed from
the politically conservative discourse of Washington and the
politically progressive discourse of Du Bois into a full-blown
apocalyptic discourse. Such a discourse would see the cultural
aesthetics of the Enlightenment radicalized into an imperialist
cult of black genius.

The political question that confronted Garvey was not
whether republican ideology is worthy of acceptance under the
colonial conditions of racial discrimination. Moreover, the question was not whether blacks in the republic of the United States
or in the commonwealth of the British empire have a universal
right to full citizenship. On these questions, Garvey was convinced of the rightness of both republican ideology and the
universal right of African Americans. The political question

was practical. Garvey's mature politics transcended the liberal-conservative and liberal-progressive politics of both Washington and Du Bois. For Garvey, the *negro problem* was global and the answer to the problem had also to be global (*Papers*, 1983, 1: 55–56).

A controlling motif in Garvey's cultural philosophy is his belief that this state of the Negro throughout the world represents the marks of deformation in African civilization. Garvey understood the African problem to be a consequence of the race's fall from preeminence among the ancient nations. This involved him in a hermeneutic of return in which the past glories of Africa are rehearsed in terms of the tragic fall of the mother of Western civilization. And civilization is associated with the progressive of mankind or the advanced civilizations of Europe, in particular the British empire. In his pre-World War I politics, Garvey's rhetoric was reminiscent of the cult of black masculinity that runs from Walker and Washington to Du Bois.

> The Negro is ignored today simply because he has kept himself backward; but if he were to try to raise himself to a higher state in the civilized cosmos, all the other races would be glad to meet him in the plane of equality and comradeship. It is indeed unfair to demand equality when one of himself has done nothing to establish the right to equality. (1:55–56)

While in his early philosophy, Garvey conceived of equality not so much as a right of nature but as a right of civil recognition, a privilege, he nevertheless believed that self-determination and self-realization are developed through a positive historical racial consciousness. He romanticized the past civilizations of Africa and their contributions to modern Western civilization, saying, "the glories of the past should tend to inspire us with courage to create a worthy future" (1:61). For Garvey, civilized idealism is captured best in the metaphor of black masculinity, "The New Man" who is fit once again "for the association of the 'gods' and the true companionship of those whose respect he lost" (1:61). Garvey insisted that "the Negro start out seriously to help himself" (1:61). By exercising self-determination, blacks will exhibit the virtues proper to civilization—namely, self-industry and racial cooperation.

In the wake of World War I, Garvey's cultural philosophy went through a modification that might well be called a transvaluation of values. It is a transition from "THE END OF PROPHECY" to "THE BEGINNING OF THE APOCALYPSE." World War I had given hope to thousands of enlisted blacks who were recruited throughout the world to fight on behalf of democracy in Europe with the hope that their own equality would result from their war efforts. "After winning the fight, winning the battle," Garvey writes in 1919, "we realize that we are without democracy; and we come before the world, therefore . . . to demand our portion of democracy; we say woe betide the man or nation who stands in the way of the negro fighting for democracy!" (1:501). In righteous indignation, Garvey turned away from the idea that political equality is a right to be earned to the idea that political equality is a human right to be demanded. Freedom had become, for Garvey, a *Divine Right* and hence, an absolute right (1:501–2).

Garvey's cultural philosophy was no longer informed by personal, perfectionist ethics, or by prophetic appeals to congress, legislators, or presidents for justice. Equality comes by revolution, imperialism, and power. Garvey articulates his imperialist outlook in the following passage.

> We are striking homewards towards Africa to make her the big Black republic, and in the making of Africa a big, black republic, what is the barrier? The barrier is the white man; and we say to the white man who now dominates Africa, that it is to his interests to clear out of Africa now, because we are coming, not as in the time of Father Abraham, 200,000 strong, but we are coming 400,000,000 strong; and we mean to re-take every square inch of the 12,000,000

square miles of African territory belonging to us by right divine. (1:502)

The quote above suggests how Garvey's turn to African imperialism and his radical transvaluations in ethics were wedded rhetorically to an apocalyptic vision. While Garvey continued to maintain an emphasis on racial pride, love, benevolence, and confraternity, his moral directives were no longer determined by a vision of cooperation with Europeans and white Americans. It is in this regard that Garvey's public theology meant an end of prophecy. No longer would appeals of blacks for justice go to the king, the president, or the government. The time had come for a great reversal. In his apocalyptic turn, everything white would become black and what was black would become white. "We have caught a new doctrine," says Garvey. "The black man is saying that everything that is pure is Black; as the white man has been saying all the time that the devil is black, and God is white, we are going to say that God is black and the devil is white" (1:505).

The cultural philosophy of African imperialism envisions the expulsion of white domination from Africa. It suggests a totalizing vision of African self-determination and the possibility of an immanent conquest of Africa, *the Land of Promise.*

> A new spirit, a new courage, has come to us simultaneously as it came to the other peoples of the world. It came to us at the same time it came to the Jew. When the Jew said, "We shall have Palestine!" the same sentiment came to us when we said, "We shall have Africa!" (2:411)

In the words "we shall have Africa," Garvey articulates a vision for a great people and empire. But to actualize this vision would take the mobilization of African masses throughout the world around this one cause, making Africa a great nation. Ironically, the model upon which imperial Africa was to be shaped were the white European and British imperialist nations. African imperialism is the mirror of European imperialism. The blackness Garvey extols is the mirror of white racial ideology. Equality would come as Africans learned the ethics of white men. "Civilization means to the Negro just what it means to the white man or any other man" (2:415). The radical implications of Garvey's politics would come to full expression when he said in 1924, "there is no law, there is no justice but power" (5:528) and "there is no prosperity, no success, no law, no justice but strength and power" (5:530). Strength and power had become, for Garvey, the virtues proper for African American cultural philosophy, for the politics of empires, and for public theology.

Garvey's African imperialism provided a third racial apologetic in African American cultural philosophy. His racial apologetic was informed neither by the accommodationist politics of Washington nor by the assimilationist politics of Du Bois. His was an apocalyptic politics informed by the new revolutionary spirit of post-World War I. As a religious critic, Garvey also differed from both Washington and Du Bois in a very important way. Washington and Du Bois continued to press their appeals for justice to the *powers that be* within the republic. And in this regard they were American jeremiads. But Garvey's African imperialism would make its appeal to a higher authority, a divinized racial community. Justice would come not from the hands of white judicial priests, but it would come in the apocalyptic fulfillment of Ethiopia's children reclaiming Africa. And in this regard, Garvey's racial apologetics signaled the end of prophecy and the beginning of the black apocalypse in African American cultural philosophy.

BEYOND CATEGORICAL RACISM AND
RACIAL APOLOGETICS

Garvey's apocalypse has not arrived; there has been no great exodus of black masses from around the world to Africa. The radical rhetoric that structured Garvey's imperialist ethic has had only marginal influence on black paramilitary insurgent movements and Islamic nationalist movements of the 1960s and 70s. It survives in the petty bourgeois intellectualism of the black aesthetic school, and in the cultic imagination of cultural Afrocentricity. Moreover, the cultural apologetics of black liberal politics from Washington and Du Bois to the civil rights movement also survives. It survives in the moralistic rhetoric of black neoconservatives and their politics of meritocracy. It also survives in the struggling voices of black progressive liberals as they try to keep the spirit of Great Society Federalism actively responsible in fair racial public policy. Both black liberal and radical politics survive without the ideological unity that was once supplied by blacks' common struggles against Jim Crow legislation and the categorical racism that legitimated it.

In categorical racism, all persons who are classified as members of a racial group are included in qualities that distinguish that group from others. Categorical racism covers every individual instance of the race, while bracketing the material, particular differences that identify individuals within the race. It invites categorical judgments about the individual members of the group. When these judgments are negative or pejorative, the group as a whole is rendered a pseudospecies.

I have tried to show how categorical racism is played out in the various cultural philosophies of European and American intellectuals. While I have focused on aesthetic and political aspects of categorical racism, David Theo Goldberg, a noted cultural critic, adequately shows its pervasive influences on historical and scientific aspects of comparative cultural anthropology (Goldberg, 1993, 29ff.). His discussion of racial aesthetics in the Enlightenment is applicable here:

> Natural qualities of beauty and perfection were supposed to be established on a priori grounds of racial membership. Aesthetic value solidified into natural law, which in the eighteenth-century was considered as compelling as the laws of nature, economics, and morality precisely because they

were all deemed to derive from the same rational basis. It is for this reason that many natural historians, biologists, and anthropologists at the time classified humankind not simply on grounds of physical criteria like size and shape, climate, or environment but according to the aesthetic value of beauty or deformity. These aesthetic values of bodily beauty were established as the mode of determining the individual's place in the racial, and therefore social, hierarchy; and perceived intellectual ability or its lack were considered to reveal inherent racial differences in mental capacity. Blacks were quite frequently represented in eighteenth-century European portrait paintings and . . . most often in subservient and demeaning fashion. . . . The racialized relations of social power are reflected in and reproduced by the aesthetics of popular portraiture of the time. (30–31)

The pervasive influences of categorical racism undergird a white racial ideology that justified the exclusion of blacks from the openings of democratic culture. The African presence in America is a racialized *other* whose blackness constitutes a fundamental natural inequality.

Categorical racism consequently gave rise to a racial apologetic in African American cultural philosophy. It is an apologetic that sought to ameliorate blacks' alienation from the progressive democratic movements of Western culture, politics, aesthetics, philosophy, and morals. The aim of racial apologetics was to overturn the negative prejudices under which white racial ideology defined black identity and to advance positive black cultural qualities in defense of African Americans' cultural assimilation. For African American cultural philosophers of the nineteenth and twentieth centuries, the integration of blacks into the cultural mainstream was preferable to isolation, expatriatism, and difference. African American historian Darlene Clark Hine explains:

I suspect that the most disturbing thing about the Fifteenth amendment from a black woman's perspective was that it allowed black men the latitude to determine the public agenda in the struggle against racism. Black men embraced the ideology of integration. Few representative black leaders, despite advocacy of different tactics and strategies, questioned the rightness of the goal of full, unfettered assimilation. This is by no means intended to ignore the movement of the thousands of African Americans who left the South in the 1880s and established scores of all-black towns on the western frontiers. I am suggesting, however, that male leaders of the millions of blacks who remained in southern states and in some northern communities differed only as to the means by which assimilation and integration were to be achieved and over what time frame. Black men from Booker T. Washington to W. E. B. Du Bois viewed the establishment of autonomous, separate organizations and institutions essentially means to an end. Of course Marcus Garvey in the early twenties and Du Bois in the thirties had denounced integrationism. But when they did so they swam against mainstream black political thought. As integrationism became the entrenched ideology and goal in the public-sphere debates, black women were increasingly silenced and overshadowed. (1993, 345)

As a counter-discourse to categorical racism, black racial apologetics reinscribed black presence in American culture as aesthetically heroic and creative and morally masculine and self-determined. Black leaders did not see these qualities as imitative of white genius; rather they regarded them as essential qualities of black genius. Black heroic genius constituted authentic black presence. A recent Du Bois biographer, Arnold Rampersad, further elaborates on this point in his discussion of *Souls of Black Folk* (1990):

In a variety of tones the narrator of *The Souls of Black Folk* relates the epic of his own soul-struggles, emerging finally as a man enduring but determined to prevail. Du Bois' self-portrait stresses the necessity of moral and psychological heroism, the qualities without which, he affirms, life is meaningless. The work ringingly affirms his faith in the strength of the African soul against which that other powerful soul, implanted by the white world, wages constant war. (88)

Black heroic genius provided twentieth century African American cultural philosophy with stable rhetorical categories for construing the historical significance of African American presence in American culture. Select passages by Howard Thurman and Dr. Martin Luther King, Jr., illustrate the point.

Thurman described African American presence in America as an epic search for identity in a nation where blacks are bound by the dilemma of "not knowing at any given moment whether they are insiders or outsiders" (1986, 88). Thurman's epic climaxes in a eulogy that celebrates the heroic qualities of black suffering under the exclusionary practices of racial discrimination and blacks' survival against cultural alienation:

Many tried to keep before their view heroes and heroines of the past to bolster a sagging self-estimate in the present. But there was ever the insinuating circumstance, the heroes failed where they themselves had failed—they were outsiders—the walls, sometimes bold and direct, often soft-spoken and indirect, were ever present.

The heroic quality of life was not missing. But the precious ingredient had never been found to protect or immunize the hero from the final assault that would send him crashing to the ground! The hero had to be a man of courage, possessing the acumen of mind and the discipline of training that could stand up under the scrutiny of the sharpest critics who guarded the citadels of power upon which society based its security, prowess, and control. In addition he must be one whose sense of community was deep in the throb of Negro life so that between his heart and theirs there would be a swinging door that no man could shut. His thinking, his feeling, and his deeds must transcend all that separates and divides. He must know hate and conquer it with love; he must know fear and conquer it with strange new courage.

As a result of a series of fortuitous circumstances there appeared on the horizon of the common life a young man who for a swift, staggering, and startling moment met the demands of the hero. . . . And his name was Martin Luther King Jr. (95)

Martin Luther King, Jr., is often described as representative of "The New Negro," says James M. Washington (1986, xv). King defined the civil rights movement in terms of black heroic genius. In the triumphs of civil rights, King saw the formation of a new revolutionary consciousness among African Americans. "Once [the African American] thought of himself as an inferior and patiently accepted injustice and exploitation. Those days are gone," says King (1986, 5). For King, the essential meaning of the civil rights movement was ultimately disclosed as an epochal threshold to a new revolutionary racial consciousness among African Americans:

Once plagued with a tragic sense of inferiority resulting from the crippling effects of slavery and segregation, the Negro has now been driven to reevaluate himself. He has come to feel that he is somebody. With this new sense of somebodiness and self-respect, a new Negro has emerged with a new sense of somebodiness and self-respect, a new Negro has emerged with a new determination to achieve freedom and human dignity whatever the cost may be. . . . There is a new Negro on the scene with a new sense of dignity and destiny. (101)

These samples from Thurman and King show how the racialized categories of the heroic, creative, masculine, and revolutionary structure authentic black consciousness in the racial apologetics of African American cultural philosophy. The success of this apologetic was owing to categorical racism, the cultural conditions of racial discrimination, the justifications of these conditions under white racial ideology, and the development of an emergent black bourgeoisie for whom Du Bois's *two souls* best captured the crisis of alienation among their black intelligentsia. Categorical racism required a counter-discourse, a black aesthetic, and a black racial ideology.

Ontological blackness is the covering term for this counter-discourse in African American cultural philosophy. It renders Du Bois's *double consciousness* a critical principle in the critique of black identity. In ontological blackness, Du Bois's *two souls* are taken as determinant boundaries in African American identity formation. Black racial identities are defined by an alienated form of self-consciousness that manifests itself in internal contradiction of loyalties and ambivalence about one's cultural heritage (Moses, 1993, 290). The ambiguities, contradictions, and conflictive racialized identities of African Americans are often regarded as the impetus for the emergent cultural genius of African Americans as they perpetually confront categorical racism.

Confrontation implies a *facing off.* However, the irony occurs in the facing off. When the two souls face each other as *lure and loathing,* within the same racialized body, then black self-consciousness is the mirror of whiteness. Commenting on this Du Boisean paradox of unresolved lure and loathing, C. Eric Lincoln writes:

> The "lure and the loathing," a romantic euphemism for black self-hatred, is the extrapolation of the Du Boisean dubiety that allegedly commits the African American to unending irresolution and self-flagellation in the fruitless effort to fully realize the "American" component of his being. The clue that such an effort is bound to end in frustration is stated clearly in Du Bois' soliloquy in *The Souls of Black*

Folk when he recognizes that the "true self-consciousness" he seeks must always be refracted through "the revelation of the other world." True self-consciousness through such a refraction is of course no self-consciousness at all, but only the reception of external projections which may well be inconsistent with any objective reality. The clue becomes the obvious when Du Bois recognizes that his soul is being measured by "the tape of a world that looks on in amused contempt and pity." (1993, 197)

Black intellectuals, such as Wilson J. Moses and Darlene Clark Hine, are asking themselves to what extent the Du Boisean representation of black self-consciousness—as alienated consciousness—is categorically disclosive of black presence in American culture and to what extent black heroic genius determines authentic black identity. Wilson J. Moses, a professor of African American studies, calls the Du Boisean dialectic into question most pointedly when he writes: "Two souls? All thinking people have more than two Souls" (1993, 289). Moses thinks that such a recognition ought to broaden African American racial discourse to confront the multiple ways that fundamental anxieties, centering around class, gender, sexuality, and ethnicity, continually condition African American identity formations.

Facing these ambiguities requires African American cultural philosophers to transcend modernity's racial consciousness, categorical racism, white racial ideology, and racial apologetics. What is required is critical discourse that refuses to reduce black identities to two souls. Such a reduction seems to Moses "like reducing oneself to two dimensions" (274). In a summary way, Darlene Clark Hine puts forward a similar sentiment. She writes:

As African American men and women of all classes . . . confront the twenty-first century there is a need for new thinking, and more inclusive and varied metaphors about black identity and the process of assimilation. The history of the American Negro is more than a history of efforts as Du Bois put it "to attain self-conscious manhood," it is simultaneously a story of the development and preservation of a dynamic, multiconscious black womanhood.

For the record, no such person as a generic Negro or a generic American exists. Inasmuch as we all experience life along axes of difference, each black or American is a person of some specific sex or sexual orientation. Each person has a certain class or social status and each belongs to what is called a "race." Here I must underscore that there is only one biological race and that is the human race. (1993, 338)

What critics like Wilson J. Moses and Darlene Clark Hine are calling for in African American cultural philosophy is a new cultural politics of difference, one that goes beyond categorical racism and racial apologetics. I join my voice to theirs.

■   ■   ■

The intention of this chapter is genealogical. Genealogies are not histories or historical explanations. They are peculiar, selective ways of making connections, mapping influences, and exposing the claims that one body (whether literal or figurative) has over another body. In most genealogies, some figures in the line of influence become central, while others recede into the background and are merely mentioned. The present discussion of categorical racism and racial apologetics is no exception. The discussion turns on the explication of categorical racism and racial apologetics in relation to white racial ideology and the classical black aesthetic. However, what is at stake in this genealogy is the subjugation of human bodies and human faces under these conceptual boundaries.

The aim of African American cultural and religious criticism is to unmask the ways that categorical racism and white racial ideology subjugate (deface) black presence in North Atlantic culture under the totality of European genius. I contend that this same iconoclastic disposition also ought to expose the ways that ontological blackness subjugates (defaces) black subjectivity under the cult of black heroic genius.

In its apologetic function, ontological blackness mirrors categorical racism. It represents categorical ways of transferring negative qualities associated with the group onto others within the group. It creates essential criteria for defining insiders and outsiders within the group. It subjugates the creative, expressive activities of blacks (whether in performance arts or literature) under the symbolism of black heroic genius. In this case, black subjectivity has internal meaning insofar as it represents the genius of the group. It makes race identity a totality that subordinates and orders internal differences among blacks, so that gender, social standing, and sexual orientations are secondary to racial identity.

Pressing beyond ontological blackness requires African American religious critics to subvert every racial discourse, including their own, that would bind black subjectivity to the totality of racial identity. But it also requires critics to advance possibilities of cultural transcendence from the binary determinants of racial apologetics. Therefore, African American cultural and religious criticism can remain open to the self-deprecating aspects of black culture as well as to the cultural fulfillment of black culture.

three

ONTOLOGICAL BLACKNESS IN
THEOLOGY

In 1969, a revolutionary moment in black American culture, James H. Cone wrote: "What is needed is not integration but a sense of worth in being black, and only black people can teach that. Black consciousness is the key to the Black man's emancipation from his distorted self-image" (1989, 19). The juxtaposition of black revolutionary consciousness (as the subject of liberation) and hope (as the ground motive of liberation) frame the argument of this chapter. The black theology project was born out of the chaos of deferred cultural fulfillment. A new revolutionary racial consciousness was ascending among an emergent educated class of black intellectuals and black theology sought to defend this revolutionary agenda.

Black theology would take its point of departure from black life and experience, which constitute the exceptional social location for a theology of black power. If white theology was viewed as an ideology of oppression, then black theology would become the ideology of liberation (127). Black theology's method is correlational. The task of the black theologian is to show the critical correlations existing between black life/experience and traditional theological categories (God, humanity, Christ, eschatology, and so forth), between black religion and black radicalism (Wilmore, 1983), and the correlations between the black church and black theology. The sources of black theology are black history, black faith, and black cultural activities. And the ultimate end of black theology is the construction of a "new black being" (134).

The argument of this chapter is that black theology constructs its new being on the dialectical structures that categorical racism and white racial ideology bequeathed to African American intellectuals (notwithstanding its claims for privileging black sources). However, the new being of black theology remains an alienated being whose mode of existence is determined by crisis, struggle, resistance, and survival—not thriving, flourishing, or fulfillment. Its self-identity is always bound by white racism and the culture of survival. The motive of transcendence from this unresolved matrix of struggle and survival recedes into the background as oppression is required for the self-disclosure of the oppressed. I suggest that as long as black theology remains determined by ontological blackness, it remains not only a crisis theology but also a theology in a crisis of legitimation.

THE BLACK THEOLOGY PROJECT

The expressive elements of black heroic genius in African American theology peaked in 1969 and the 70s in the black theology project. James H. Cone is its unsurpassed representative. In the preface to his 1986 edition of *A Black Theology of Liberation* (1991), first published in 1970, Cone framed his discourse under the idea of ontological blackness. Cone suggests that the theological problem for blacks as well as the entire problem of American culture is subsumed under white racism. And in the matrix of black existence and white racism, Cone explicates the meaning of ontological blackness in terms of an emergent collective black revolutionary consciousness (23). The critical task of black theologians is to disclose the "essential religious and theological meaning" of this new black collective consciousness in light of the black experience, black history, and black culture. Black experience is a "totality of black existence in a white world where babies are tortured, women are raped, and men are shot. . . . The black experience is existence in a system of white racism" (24). Such an experiential matrix is symbolized by Cone as a *Symbolic Blackness* (7). It expresses itself in:

> The power to love oneself precisely because one is black and a readiness to die if whites try to make one behave otherwise. It is the sound of James Brown singing, "I'm Black and I'm Proud" and Aretha Franklin demanding "respect." The black experience is catching the spirit of blackness and loving it. It is hearing black preachers speak of God's love in spite of the filthy ghetto, and black congregations responding Amen, which means that they realize that ghetto existence is not the result of divine decree but of white inhumanity. (25)

The black theology project seeks to disclose the essential meanings of black faith in the black God revealed in the black Christ from the perspective of the black experience. Cone writes in a later work:

> When I speak of black faith, I am referring only secondarily to organized religion and primarily to black people's collective acknowledgment of the spirit of liberation in their midst, a Spirit who empowers them to struggle for freedom even though the odds are against them. This is the historical matrix out of which my hermeneutical perspective has been formed. (1986, 43)

The essential meaning of the black collective consciousness (ontological blackness) is the resolve of two cultural motifs, both of which are reconfigurations of the classical black aesthetic: black survivalist culture and black revolutionary self-assertion.

Survival "is a way of life for the black community," says Cone.
And C. Eric Lincoln and Lawrence Mamiya would write twenty
years after Cone, in their monumental work on the black
church, that black "culture is the sum of the options for creative
survival" (1990, 3). "Black theology is a theology of survival,"
Cone argued, "because it seeks to interpret the theological significance of the being of a community whose existence is threatened by the power of non-being" (1991, 16). Moreover, it seeks
to elicit the essential theological meaning of black self-assertion
as "an event of liberation taking place in the black community
in which blacks recognize that it is incumbent upon them to
throw off the chains of white oppression by whatever means
they regard as necessary" (5). And, for Cone, any means necessary might mean "attacking the enemy of black humanity by
throwing a Molotov cocktail into a white-owned building and
watching it go up in flames" (25). Although such a position
seems revolutionary enough, such an act of racial frustration is
not likely to transact cultural fulfillment.

It is only insofar as Cone extends these essentialized meanings of the new black revolutionary consciousness to black cultural productions themselves that ontological blackness
climaxes in the absurdity that "the black experience is possible
only for black persons":

> [The black experience] means having natural hair cuts,
> wearing African dashikis, and dancing to the sound of
> Johnny Lee Hooker or B. B. King, knowing that no matter
> how hard whitey tries there can be no real duplication of
> black "soul." Black soul is not learned; *it comes from the totality
> of black experience*, the experience of carving out an existence
> in a society that says you do not belong. (25; emphasis mine)

For Cone, the essential theological meanings of black experience, black history, and black culture—all of which represent
the black collective consciousness—emerge in a symbolic expressive play of the heroic survivalist culture of the black com-

munity, the pain and joy it derives from "reacting to whiteness and affirming blackness" and "the mythic power inherent in [its historical] symbols for the present revolution against white racism" (28). When the theological meaning of ontological blackness is accented, black theology approaches an identification of black culture with the Christ event in which "God's revelation comes to us in and through the cultural situation of the oppressed" (28). And black culture (art, music, literature, and theology) is the expressive vehicle of black liberation by the black messiah.

A number of problems plagued Cone's project from the beginning. These problems centered around the relation of black theology to the black churches. Early critics, particularly those who pressed internal criticisms as black church theologians, asked how black theology could be a theology of the black churches if it fundamentally disentangles itself from the creeds and confessions, as well as the liturgical practices that structure the black churches. To some, black theology appeared to posit within itself a revolutionary consciousness that looked more like the mirror of white racism and less like an expression of the evangelical gospel that characterized most black churches. Was black theology, then, an academic project in theology rather than an ecclesiastical project? Others asked, in what sense could black theology be black since its theological method was derived from white European theologians, notably Karl Barth and Paul Tillich, and European philosophers such as Albert Camus and Jean Paul Sartre?

In subsequent writings throughout the 70s and 80s, Cone tried to answer many of the problems that center around the relation of black theology to the black churches and to black culture in books such as *A Black Theology of Liberation* (1970), *The Spirituals and the Blues* (1972), *God of the Oppressed* (1975), and *Speaking the Truth* (1986). The fundamental difficulty lies in Cone's call for the radical disentanglement of black theology from white theology and European religious sources.

Cone's radically oppositional rhetoric leaves him with this dilemma: he could either capitulate his claims for exceptionalism in the production of black theology by acknowledging the indebtedness of black theology to the west European manuscript tradition in the theological formation of the black churches, or he might insist on the radical disjunction of black theology from European sources and remain a theologian alienated from the theology of the churches and their evangelical roots. Cone chose the latter. He attempted to overcome his academic alienation from the black churches by emphasizing the necessity of black sources for the construction of black theology. But this apologetic preoccupation with black sources creates more contradictions in the project than it solves.

Most of Cone's problems center around the category of symbolic blackness. Cone's problems are matters of internal contradiction. First, black theology, as Cone formulated it, risks self-referential inconsistency when it sees itself as radically oppositional to white racism and white theology. Because Cone collapses metaphysics into ontology, blackness is reified into a totality or a unity of black experience. At the same time, blackness is regarded as symbolic, so that anyone who can participate in its meaning can also be said to be black (1990, 9). However, black theology exceptionally circumscribes the meaning of symbolic blackness in terms of black oppression and suffering.

The difficulty arises here: (a) blackness is a signification of ontology and corresponds to black experience. (b) Black experience is defined as the experience of suffering and rebellion against whiteness. Yet (c) both black suffering and rebellion are ontologically created and provoked by whiteness as a necessary condition of blackness. (d) Whiteness appears to be the ground of black experience, and hence of black theology and its new black being. Therefore, while black theology justifies itself as radically oppositional to whiteness, it nevertheless requires whiteness, white racism, and white theology for the self-disclosure of its new black being and its legitimacy. In this way, black theology effectively renders whiteness identifiable with what is of ultimate concern. "Our ultimate concern is that which determines our being or not being," says Tillich (1967, 14).

The cogency of black theology, in its classical formulation, also appears performatively contradictory. Cone defined blackness in terms of Tillich's semiotics (1990, 7). On Tillich's terms, then, symbolic blackness must point to something other than itself. According to Tillich, revelatory word-symbols have a basic correlation to the ultimate mystery signified by the symbol. However, the symbolic correlation of our ordinary language and ultimate mystery is asyntotic. Thus, while theological words are not identifiable with ultimate mystery, they nevertheless may have "a denotative power that points through the ordinary meaning to us." They also have an "expressive power which points through ordinary expressive possibilities of language to the unexpressible and its relations to us," says Tillich (1967, 124).

Whether denotatively or expressively, on Tillich's account, revelatory word-symbols reflexively point beyond their ordinary meanings to the unexpressible. Therefore, theological symbols approximate what is of ultimate concern but are not identifiable with ultimate concern. "When speaking of the ultimate, of being and meaning, ordinary language brings it down to the level of the preliminary, the conditioned, the finite, thus muffling its revelatory power," says Tillich (124). Theological symbols are idolatrous when they are taken for the ground of being or nonbeing.

In black theology, blackness has become a totality of meaning. It cannot point to any transcendent meaning beyond itself without also fragmenting. Because black life is fundamentally determined by black suffering and resistance to whiteness (the power of nonbeing), black existence is without the possibility of transcendence from the blackness that whiteness created. Without transcendence from the determinancy of whiteness, black theology's promise of liberation remains existentially a function of black self-consciousness (to see oneself as black, free, and self-determined). However, since as Cone argues it is whiteness, white racism, and white theology that threatens the nonbeing of blacks, the promise of black liberation remains bracketed both existentially and politically.

Existentially, the new black being remains bound by whiteness. Politically, it remains unfulfilled because blackness is ontologically defined as the experience of suffering and survival. Any amelioration of these essential marks of blackness performatively contradicts ontological blackness in black theology. Insofar as it is predicated ontologically on symbolic blackness, black theology remains alienated from black interests in not only surviving against suffering but also thriving, flourishing, and obtaining cultural fulfillment.

Subsequent projects of thinkers such as Dwight Hopkins, James Evans, and womanist thinkers, such as Katie Cannon, Jacquelyn Grant, and Delores Williams, have tried to reassure the ecclesiastical and public relevancy of black theology. In the remaining pages of this chapter, I make clear how these subsequent formulations of the black theology project differ from the classical formulation but, at the same time, remain under the burden of ontological blackness. The decisive turn occurs in these later theologians' intentions to reassure the exceptional and essential sources legitimizing the project under *the hermeneutics of return* to black sources and the expansion of experiential matrices for rethinking ontological blackness in light of black women's experience.

"The hermeneutics of return," as I retrieve the idea from Said (1993, xii–xiii), is a narrative return to distinctively black sources for the purpose of establishing and reassuring the legitimacy of black theology in a postrevolutionary context. The theological gaze here returns to African traditional religions and slave narratives, autobiography, and folklore in order to assure the vitality of the black church (church theology) and the cultural solidarities that transcend the individualism that drives our market culture and morality, and rob the black community of moral vitality. The hermeneutics of return is a decisive element of African American fundamental theology. As a function of fundamental theology, hermeneutics is therefore prolegomenon to African American constructive theology.

Dwight N. Hopkins has been at the forefront of this fundamental theology. In his recent book, *Shoes That Fit Our Feet: Sources for a Constructive Black Theology* (1993), Hopkins attempts to play out the systematic implications of *slave theology* for the black theology project. Hopkins gives several significations for the sort of return he proposes for constructive black theology. The return is at once to *slave theology* and *bush arbor theology*. Yet as I shall show presently, both sources are attributive to black theology in such a way that it is not clear whether they are *sources* for a constructive black theology or the *product* of constructive black theology. Slave theology and African American religious experience are hybrids. Slave theology is the synthesis of "white Christianity with the remains of African religions under slavery," says Hopkins (1993, 15). As his argument goes, African slaves maintained enough residual aspects, or what Hopkins calls *remains,* of their former religions to establish a historically effective slave religion. This religion was preserved and transmitted in an invisible institution, among bushes and trees away from the eyes and ears of white and black guardians. In that institution, these *remains* achieved some measure of coherence and a regulative content. However, one of the problems in understanding Hopkins's argument is that while slave theology is fundamentally a religious hybrid, the individuated elements (African traditional religions, on the one side, and white Christianity, on the other side) are unidentifiable from the theological content of black theology.

Let us look more closely at Hopkins's argument. Hopkins argues that "enslaved Africans, the majority coming from the African West Coast, brought a distinct perception of God to North America" (16). And "African traditional religions described their ultimate divinity as the High God" (16). Hopkins then suggests that there is a correlation between the High God (who has no name in Hopkins's discourse) and Western "theological" notions of omnipresence, omnipotence, transcendence, and immanence. However, the correlation Hopkins proposes turns out to be one between the High God of African traditional religions and Israel's God.

Hopkins sees other correlations between African traditional religions and the Hebrew God when he compares cosmologies in which the earth and human flourishing are regarded as actions of the compassion and care of the High God and Yahweh:

> African indigenous religions believe in a God who cares; some call God "the Compassionate One"; others see "the God of Pity," who rescues victims in need. Even more, God is kind and "looks after the case of the poor man." In fact, God is the main hope of the poor in society. As Guardian and Keeper, God is named "the protector of the poor" by some African traditional religions. They further specify that "there is a Saviour and only he can keep our lives." As Judge, God metes out justice, punishment, and retribution. Similarly, God displays protectiveness by avenging injustice. God is a divinity of partiality to the victim; God sides with the political powerlessness of society's injured. (17)

A third correlation is also proposed in what Hopkins regards as a theological anthropology. These religions are shown to share a "dynamic and interdependent relation between the individual and the community" (17). And this correlation justifies the opposition of black theology to *individualism*.

> African religions gave rise to a dynamic interplay between community and individual. Whatever happened to the communal gathering affected the individual; whatever happened to the individual had an impact on the community. Such a theological view of humanity cuts across bourgeois notions of white Christianity's individualism and "me-first-ism." It seeks to forge a group solidarity and identity, beginning with God, proceeding through the ancestors to the community and immediate family and continuing even to

the unborn. One cannot be a human being unless one becomes a part of, feels a responsibility to, and serves the community. To preserve the community's well-being (through liberation) in African religions is to preserve the individual's well-being (through salvation). Thus salvation and liberation become a holistic individual-collective and personal-systemic ultimate concern. (17)

Hopkins argues that there are possible correlations between the High God of African traditional religions and the Hebrew God at the levels of both formal and moral utterances. And there are possible correlations between the formal and moral utterances concerning humanity at the level of theological anthropology. However, Hopkins has the burden of showing that there is a correlation between the *remains* of African traditional religions, *Africanism(s)* and *slave religion*. He must also show that the elements in correspondence are genetically independent for a successful argument for hybridity. He argues that the biblical faith of the slaves effects the synthesis:

> Enslaved Africans took the remnant of their traditional religious structures and meshed them together with their interpretation of the Bible. All of this occurred in the "Invisible Institution," far away from the watchful eyes of white people. Only in their own cultural idiom and political space could black slaves truly worship God. (18)

Bush arbor theology (the theology slaves created hidden among bushes and trees away from the eyes and ears of their masters) signifies a distinctive discursive site for the formation of a slave theology. Hopkins argues that among trees and bushes, slaves achieved "a remarkable clarity concerning the cultural dimension of their theology" (19). And the distinctive formation of their religious experience was materially manifest in ecstatic religious expressions and a political space from which they defined their humanity and established creative forms of resistance (19). Slave theology defines the content of its faith in terms of the egalitarian principle, absolute justice, and divine preference for the poor. Its content echoes both incarnational and resurrection triumphalism; and the mark of authenticity in religious experience is religious immediacy.

When I examine the claims that Hopkins makes for slave religion as a hybrid religion, I am left asking whether the hermeneutics of narrative return does not introduce more ambiguities and contradictions into Hopkins's project than it solves. Two lines of argument seem warranted: an examination of whether the coherence of Hopkins's project is compromised by committing a performative contradiction, and an examination of whether the project's legitimacy depends on a viciously circular mode of reasoning that commits hermeneutical violence not only to the African sources but also to the narrative sources. On the first charge, for all of Hopkins's talk about privileging African sources as an effective means for reassuring the legitimacy of black theology, these sources seem to fall out of or are simply consumed into Hebraic-Christian utterances. That is, so-called Africanisms are unidentifiable from the biblical utterances of Christian slaves. And instead of slave religion manifesting a hybridity, Hopkins's African slaves baptize the African gods into Hebrew faith. Therefore, Hopkins violates his principle of correlation by collapsing correlation into identification, since African religions collapse into biblical faith.

In order to explicate the biblical faith of the slaves, Hopkins has to show how the High God(s) of African traditional religions, tending to be *deus otiosus,* is identifiable with the Hebrew God of slave religions without also committing violence against the former God(s). Failure to demonstrate correlation constitutes a performative contradiction. Hopkins's argument for hybridity collapses in a performative contradiction for several reasons. Hopkins begs the question of whether the belief systems of African traditional religions are translatable (notwithstanding whatever family resemblances may exist between them and slave religion) into the languages of Hebrew/Christian faith without also committing violence against traditional religions.

Hopkins also does not show how the differences already signaled in the notion of African traditional *religions* (plural) are reducible to the sort of categorical simplicities which he calls *Africanisms*. Hopkins calls these categories *remains*. But the misnomer seems ironically quite appropriate. For in the interest of forcing not only a correlation but also an identification of African traditional religions with slave religion, Hopkins has his slave theologians carrying the *remains* of their African gods into their invisible institution and disposing of the *remains* in the inauguration of slave religion. The performative contradiction renders the return to African traditional religions a moot point if, in the end, there are no recognizable differences that would count as independent sources for black theology.

This brings me to my second criticism: that Hopkins's hermeneutics of narrative return ends up justifying the black theology project by a vicious circularity of reasoning that renders the legitimacy of slave religion coterminous with black theology and the legitimacy of black liberation theology coterminous with slave religion. When comparing the utterances properly ascribed to the slave narratives with those characteristic of the black theology project, there appears to be no significant differences that would suggest that the latter (black theology) is effectively indebted to the former sources (African traditional religion and slave theology). Both antecedent sources tend to be identified as liberation utterances. This is to say that there appears to be no difference between a source (antecedent) and its effect (consequent).

The slave narratives are rendered as just so much *proto-black liberation theology*. At its best, this is an anachronism, and at its worst, this is hermeneutical violence for the sake of reassuring the identity of the black theology project by grounding it in authentic African American religious experience. By identifying the legitimacy of black theology with that of slave religion (authentic African American religious experience and practices), Hopkins *connotatively* overcomes one of the problems that has plagued the black theology project from its inception: How is black theology an authentic expression of the black churches and their theology, and not the ideological invention of black middle-class academic theologians (mostly heterosexual males) seeking to come to terms with their alienation from the everyday, routinized functions of the churches and their members?

My criticisms try to disclose intentions in the hermeneutics of return that distinguish the recent emphasis in the black theology project from its classical formulation in the 70s. I contend that the controlling intention is to reassure, in contemporary African American public life, the ideological position of the black theology project. In other words, the return to black sources is attributive to an ideological function that is culturally apologetic. It is apologetic insofar as black theology must assure its relevance for African American public life as a project that effectively contributes to the formation of a contemporary black cultural consciousness. Its cultural relevance is not self-evident. The *return* is also an attempt to place the black theology project in solidarity with the pressing problems of the urban underclass and its culture of poverty, and to construct a position that can effectively speak to the crisis of black nihilism and its culture of violence.

The hermeneutics of return projects a grand narrative that evokes a great cloud of witnesses whose heroic legacy of survival, resistance, and hope can mediate the fragility of African American public life today and bind together our alienated generation that is so much in need of a heroic black faith. But the consequence of such a hermeneutic is that whatever claims are made for African American identity in terms of black subjectivity, these are subsumed under a black collective consciousness definable in terms of black faith. So not only are the *remains* of the African gods disposed of under the totalizing hermeneutics of black theology, but black subjectivity itself is also subjugated under the totality of black faith.

The recent systematic theology by James H. Evans, Jr., *We Have Been Believers: An African American Systematic Theology* (1992), is another attempt to reassure the project of black theology in our postmodern context of African American cultural life. Like Hopkins, Evans also continues to legitimize the project of black academic theology almost singularly in terms of ontological blackness and a cult of black heroic genius. Evans's project is also fundamentally justified in terms of a hermeneutic of return in which theology is primarily a church-dependent discourse that "is essentially the church's response to the autobiographical impulse, and it grows out of the need to proclaim with authority and commitment the identity and mission of the church in the world" (1992, 1).

However, a problem of academic black theology is its tendency toward alienation from the existential pathos and crises of the church as a community. The primary directive of Evans's book is to suggest ways in which the alienation of professional black theologians from church members can be overcome and how their mutual relation can be "strengthened so that it becomes clear that black theology is rooted in the faith of the church and that the faith of the church is given intellectual clarity and expression in black theology" (1).

Such clarity is predicated on hermeneutics more than on ritual performances, which are routinized in the everyday practices of the church. African American theology "requires a praxeological commitment to the community of faith" (1). And the faith that occupies the black theologian's tasks is that which African Americans *constructed* out of their unprecedented experience of African chattel slavery. In this context,

> They created distinctive ways of conceptualizing and speaking about ultimate concerns. Black theology is a continuation of that discursive tradition. Therefore, African-American theological development can be best understood as the convergence of an African-derived world view, the complexities of the experience of slavery, oppression, sur-

vival, rebellion, and adjustment in the New World, and the encounter with the biblical text. These realities shaped the African-American intellect and spirit. (2)

African American theology is grounded both by the theologian's recognition that his or her project is historically derivative from the economy of slavery and also expressive of the passions, feelings, and rationality that constitutes African-American Christianity.

Already some of the marks of the classical black aesthetic begin to resurface as the creative matrix from which black theology's self-understanding occurs. Through ecstatic reason, black theology correlates the economy of slavery and the heroic impetuses of survival, rebellion, and adjustment with Christian faith. Ecstatic reason is privileged as a distinctive mark of black rationality. It connects the project of black theology with the classical black aesthetics. As Evans puts it, an authentic African American theology must be "in touch with the 'guts' of Black religion. Without this quality, it would forfeit its claim to authenticity" (2). While black theology must have some occupation with "formal, self-conscious, systematic attempt[s] to interpret that faith," its mode of conceptualization is regarded as oppositional, nonlinear, and non-Western. The black theology project is not only epistemologically oppositional in its Afrocentric ideology. As an Afrocentric discourse, black theology is ontologically oppositional. The marks of Western ontology are the devaluing of community, the idolization of individuality, and "private property and individual rights as the basis of social and political organization." In distinction from these essential marks, Evans says that:

> The cultural matrix of the African tended to affirm the infinite worth of the African as a human being in relation to other human beings and under the auspices of a benevolent creator God. The community (the no longer living, the living, and the yet to be born) was affirmed as the basic social

unit and the social frame work in which the individual was defined. All creation, including nature, was seen as infused with the spiritual presence of God. (5)

What fundamentally guides the "hermeneutics of return" to black sources among the recent black theologians? Evans wants black theology to speak to the problems of contemporary black Christianity—namely, the threat of black cultural fragility and nihilism. On the one side, African Americans are caught in a crisis of faith in which they "struggle with the pull of a secular materialistic, hedonistic, narcissistic, and pessimistic culture." And on the other side, they also struggle to "experience, to varying degrees, the magnetic hold of a spiritual, integrated, communal, and hopeful, counter-culture" of black faith (6). The oppositional tension between nihilism and faith tends to push Evans normatively to affirm and reassure the communal focus in black theology and to minimize individuality.

The legitimacy for such a focus is found in the hermeneutics of narrative return. The kernel beliefs that identify African American religious faith involve a selective retrieval of the *canonical story* of God's divine interventions into the affairs of oppressors in order to effect the liberation of the oppressed in both the exodus and the Christ events. But there is also a selective reception of "folk stories" that drives black theologians to the slave narratives. The heart of these stories centers on their "fears, frustrations and struggle as well as the determination for freedom from existential anxiety, political oppression, and cultural exploitation that constitutes our experience" (7). The theologian as storyteller has a difficult task of overcoming the vicious circularity between oppression and liberation. The black theologian has to reassure the canonical gospel story as an effective liberating story in the context of black suffering. One would hope therefore that suffering can be ameliorated or transcended. At the same time, liberation is the correlate of black experience, but black experience is essentially the experience of unrelenting crisis. The oppression-liberation circle remains viciously closed to cultural transcendence.

Although Hopkins and Evans try to reassure the black theology project in terms of an Afrocentric narrative return, it remains a crisis theology in two senses. First, it is a theology of crisis insofar as it identifies ontological blackness with *black experience* and black experience as the experience of suffering and black rebellion. Where either term (suffering or rebellion) is existentially mitigated or ameliorated so that suffering and rebellion are no longer the *way of life* for black people, then the ontological matrix of such a theology must enter into a crisis of legitimacy. This is the second sense in which black theology is a theology in a crisis of legitimation. It is a theology in crisis insofar as social and cultural elements of differentiation genuinely occur among African Americans, which are sufficient to call into question any reasonable assent to such ideological totalities as *the black church, the black faith,* or *the black sacred cosmos.*

Where radical differentiation occurs among African Americans, such ideological totalities are relativized by a pluralism of quasi-religious and not so religious organizations (street gangs, black gay and lesbian clubs, military service, fraternities and sororities). They are relativized by a multitude of faith traditions including non-Christian ones (Judaism, traditional orthodox Islam, African traditional religions, and new religions). And they are relativized by the plurality of world and life views held by African Americans who occupy varying social positions of class, gender, sex, and ethnicity. Under such differentiations, suffering, rebellion, and survival cannot be categorically descriptive of black experience. Many African Americans experience privileges and benefits of social mobilization within black culture itself. To make suffering, rebellion, and survival essential marks of black existence, it seems to me, trivializes the nature of oppression many blacks genuinely experience by the absurdity that anyone who is black is also oppressed.

Both Hopkins and Evans remain honest in their intentions to reassure the viability of the black faith in our market culture by privileging black community over black subjectivity. As a community of resistance, survival, and rebellion, however, the black community subjugates black subjectivity under ontological blackness. Since ontological blackness is identifiable with black experience, it is defined by and coterminous with black resistance and black suffering. Black theology—both in its classical and Afrocentric varieties—fails to show how cultural transcendence over white racism is possible. It also fails to disclose what forms existential amelioration of black suffering and resistance will take. If suffering and resistance and white racism are ontologically constitutive of black life, faith, and theology, then transcendence from ontological blackness puts at risk the cogency of black theology.

THE CHALLENGE OF WOMANIST THEOLOGY

One of the greatest challenges facing the integrity of the black theology project is womanist theology. Themes presented in the work of theologians such as Katie Cannon (1988), Jacquelyn Grant (1989), and Delores Williams (1993) not only form shared rhetorical matrices for the production of future womanist theologies, they also form a constellation of values. In the end, we shall have to consider whether these values are successful in mitigating the aporias of black theology, which are created by black theologians' commitments to ontological blackness. Womanist theology poses several challenges for rethinking black theology.

Womanist theology attempts to negotiate the legitimation crisis of black theology both in its classical and Afrocentric variety. When it makes gender along with race and class a constitutive category of criticism, womanist theology makes regulative a womanist consciousness that includes within itself the privilege of difference. Therefore, theoretically, it can mediate the impasses of binary oppositions that often subjugate black women's experience. Such oppositions are those between whiteness/blackness, oppressors/oppressed, and community/personality.

Delores Williams sees mediatorial possibilities as constitutive of what Alice Walker means by *womanist*. Williams is worth quoting at length:

> Walker identifies a womanist as Black or of other color. Cone has shown well enough how Black people's color has been the basis upon which many white Americans have judged Black people to be subhuman. Walker lifts up Black women involved in the single-parenting act of passing on advice to the female child. The relationship between mother and child in a single-parent household is not valued as the proper circumstance out of which "normal" and psychologically healthy children can come. These kinds of relationships and family life are devalued. Needless to say, American culture does not value the advice women give. Walker, in her description of a womanist, challenges stereotypical ideas devaluating Black women. She describes a womanist as "responsible . . . in charge . . . serious." This challenges the stigma of "childlike," "girlish," and "frivolous," which patriarchal and demonarchial social attitudes assign to Black women. According to Walker, a womanist loves men and women sexually or nonsexually. This challenges those who devalue the humanity of lesbian women. A womanist defines universality in terms of an array of skin colors. This gives intrinsic value to all skin colors: "brown, pink, and yellow" as well as "white, beige, and black." Walker describes Black women's love in terms of dance, the moon, the spirit, love, food, roundness, struggle, the folks, and love of themselves as women. This affirms the cultural elements through which black women express their humanity. To devalue any of this understanding of a womanist is to devalue Black women's womanhood, to devalue their humanity, to be guilty of sin—the sin that denies that Black women's humanity is in the image of God as is all humanity. (1993, 145–46)

Williams sees in the promise of womanist prose an inclusive vision for reinscribing black women's consciousness beyond the ontological categories of black theology. So the promise of racial and cultural mediation seems included in the womanist definition. Williams rightly sees that womanist theologians add not only challenges to the hegemony of black, male clergy over legitimacy claims in African American religion and theology. But the question remains whether their gender challenges contextually and hermeneutically transcend the fundamental orientations of ontological blackness that structure the black theology project without at the same time vitiating their real interests.

Contextually, womanist theology makes regulative a comprehensive experiential matrix for the analysis of African American life. This experiential matrix is a tri-modal configuration of black oppression: racism, sexism, and classism. Therefore, womanist theology poses a challenge to the binary matrices that have driven prior racial discourse in African American religion and theology. However, it is evident that womanist theology contextually remains bound by ontological blackness, since the defining category is black oppression.

At the contextual level, womanist theologians tend to accent themes of cultural domination and alienation as vitiating cultural fulfillment. Black women's *womanhood* is devalued by white racism and sexism. The hegemony of white, male cultural elitism and black, male elitism remain hegemonic. Domination is not the only attending sign of black women's experience. In addition, there is also alienation. The general context for womanist theological writings tends to be not only that of pervasive racism and its discriminatory effects resulting in the domination of white over black. But the context is also one of alienation from the goods of democratic society.

Katie Cannon puts it in these terms:

> I first began pondering the relationship between faith and ethics as a schoolgirl while listening to my grandfather teach

the central affirmations of Christianity within the context of a racially segregated society. My community of faith taught me that the principles of God's universal parenthood which engendered a social, intellectual and cultural ethos, embracing the equal humanity of all people. Yet, my city, state, and nation declared it a punishable offense against the laws and mores for Blacks and whites "to travel, eat, defecate, wait, be buried, make love, play, relax, and even speak together, except in the stereotyped context of master and servant interaction. (1988, 1)

While Cannon stresses the ways that white racism determines black women's experience, Jacquelyn Grant emphasizes the internal duplicity that is signified by white racism. She attends to the complicity of white-female privilege and its legitimation of black women's oppression. In *White Women's Christ and Black Women's Jesus* (1989), Grant tends to emphasize the triple oppression of black women as a fundamental differentiating precedent for constructive womanist theology. This triple cluster allows Grant to press charges of white women's complicity in black women's oppression. Grant argues that "feminist theology is inadequate for two reasons: it is White and racist" (1989, 195). Therefore, it cannot be a viable source of womanist discourse, because it cannot disentangle itself from the determinants of biological pedigree. Neither can it disentangle itself from the legacy of the white manuscript tradition in theology (195). "Although there are sharp differences among feminist theologians," Grant nevertheless argues that "they are *all* of the *same* race and the influence of their race has led them to similar sources for the definition of their perspectives on the faith" (195; Grant's emphasis). Grant's critique of feminist theology is that it is not only white but also racist. This identification of whiteness and racism is for her categorical. Therefore, it is a matter of definition.

Grant's argument depends on her accepting a definition of racism that is categorically predicated on the supremacist action of a dominant racial group on a minor and subjugated racial group (199 ff.). The logic of Grant's argument is that racism is categorically a function of the systemic behavior of the dominant racial group—namely, whites. Since white women are entailed in the privileges of white racism, white feminist theology is by definition also racist.

What is at stake in Grant's categorical argument in distinction from Cannon's relative silence about white feminist complicity in black women's oppression? For Grant, the issue is black women allowing whites, in this case white women, to define black women's experience in terms of white women's racial and class interests.

Grant holds that whatever interests black women may share with white women in terms of gender identification, the privileges that attend to whiteness at racial and class levels negate white feminists' genuine interest in the liberation of black women from black women's tri-modal oppression. The historic disparities between white and black women sexually under the economy of slavery and segregation, Grant argues, "have created a gulf between these women, that White feminists' common assumptions that all women are in the same situation with respect to sexism is difficult to understand when history so clearly tells us a different story" (196).

At the contextual level, their triple experience of oppression in terms of race, gender, and class provides womanist theologians an angle of vision that anticipates some promise of transcendence over the burdens of ontological blackness. Black existence, whether male or female, is bound by unprecedented suffering and survival. Yet it appears, at least on Grant's argument, that womanists' demands and claims for exceptionalism require the stability of ontological blackness for the legitimacy of their project. In the case of Grant, ontological blackness results in a categorical racial reductionism that morally diminishes her capacity to distinguish friends from enemies.

By making racism categorical and identifiable with whiteness, Grant effectively reduces the logic of womanist exceptionalism formally to the reductio ad absurdum that every black woman is also a womanist. Presently, we shall see how one African American theologian, Cheryl J. Sanders, challenges the logic of Grant's racial reductionism. Womanist claims for contextual exceptionalism are defective when they are based on ontological blackness. More importantly, such racial reasoning also lessens the possibilities of transcendence promised experientially in Walker's womanist connotations. In this regard, Grant appears to be a mitigated womanist theologian.

At the hermeneutical level of womanist theological criticism, womanist theology tends to privilege not only traditional biblical/theological manuscript sources but also narratives, autobiographies, and black women's writings as primary sources for theology. By giving centrality to black women's writings, however, womanist theologians make a significant advancement on the black theology project by adding not merely a neglected dimension of discourse but adding discourse that has been subjugated under black-male elitism. Womanist hermeneutics takes its defining materials from black women's literature and slave narratives to disclose ancestral wisdom. For womanist theologians, these sources function as black women's wisdom literature.

Like the hermeneutical return of classical black theology and its recent Afrocentric variety, womanist narrativism inevitably ends up reassuring its project in terms of ontological blackness. The ironic consequence is that a discourse predicated on self-definition and black women's difference remains bound by the specter of black masculinity and its cult of black heroic genius. Their stress lies on the unprecedented evidence of black women's capacities for survival under unprecedented suffering. Black women's sources tend to be used toward disclosing the heroic, survivalist genius of black women.

The turn to black women's literature tends to serve the apologetic intentions of buttressing the exceptionalist claims made for womanist theology. A few representational passages must suffice here rather than close readings. "Black women have created and cultivated a set of ethical values that allow them to prevail against the odds, with moral integrity, in their ongoing participation in the white-male-capitalist value system," says Katie Cannon (1988, 75ff.). She continues: "The best available literary repository for this underground treasury of values is the Black women's literary tradition" (75). This literary treasure ought not to be identified strictly with black women's novels or poetry. But the womanist narrative return includes writings drawn from autobiographers, ex-slave interviewers, journalists, and black women essayists. Although there are many available sources from which womanist theologians draw for their project, their historical retrievals are governed by survivalist intentions.

From these various sources, womanist theologians engage in a selective retrieval of materials which in turn reinforce a constellation of values that identify them with the womanist project. The following represents a typical constellation of figures: Maria Stewart, Harriet Tubman, Sojourner Truth, Harriet Jacobs, Mary Prince, Louisa Picuet, Mattie Jackson, Zora Hurston, Alice Walker, and Toni Morrison. They form a constellation of *sassy* witnesses whose stories of suffering and whose accounts of survival and resistance are representational of womanist consciousness.

Clarice Martin sees in the strategy of reiterative hermeneutics a theological methodology that is intricately expressive of black women's spiritual autobiography. Reiterative hermeneutics is a strategy that involves "a declarative rehearsal, a reiteration of the ways in which God has delivered, rescued, transformed, and re-empowered the self or the community in the face of suffering and calamity," says Martin (1993, 28):

> African-American autobiographies typically include expressed desires for full and uninhibited self-actualization, a critique of external national conditions, and an interweaving of individual and communal consciousness. It is the African American "spiritual" autobiography that contains

some of the most poignantly stirring recitations and reitera-
tions of the conviction that God sustains life as it exists in a
whirlwind of chaos. God rescues, delivers, and succors the
sufferer and besieged sojourner on the road to life. (28)

Black women's autobiographies are representational of "radical
uses of traditional forms of spirituality," says Martin. Such a
radicalism led black women "'to question fearlessly what they
perceived to be illegitimate authority to wage war against' an
intemperate, sexist, and slave holding society" (29).

Womanist hermeneutics aims at reassuring the humanity of
black women by disclosing forms of false and illusionary consciousness among black women and in the black community.
"Only by attending to Black women's feelings and experiences,
understanding and reflection, judgement and evaluation about
their situation," M. Shawn Copeland argues, "can we adequately challenge the stereotypes about Black women—
especially stereotypes that coalesce around that most popular
social convention of female sexuality, the 'cult of true womanhood'" (1993, 111). Positively stated, the existential import of
womanist hermeneutics is to disclose an authentic consciousness
of black womanhood that speaks to "black women's accounts of
pain and anguish, of their individual and collective struggle to
grasp and manage, rather than be managed by their suffering"
(111, 118).

There is much that is commendable about womanist theology. It reminds us that black women's experience is complex
and often neglected in the interest of racial criticism. It is useful
for disclosing forms of consciousness that subjugate black
women's subjectivity and personality under the totality of race
and black masculinity. Yet in its hermeneutics, womanist theology suffers the contradictions of ontological blackness. It proposes the privilege of self-definition. Yet ontological blackness
binds the discourse almost exclusively and exceptionally to suffering and resistance.

If suffering and resistance continue to have a totalizing function in womanist theological discourse as they do in classical black theology and Afrocentric theologies, on what does transcendence depend? At what point do thriving and flourishing enter the equation of suffering and resistance? An existence that is bound existentially only by the dimensions of struggle and resistance or survival, it seems to me, constitutes a less than fulfilling human existence. We all want more than to survive: that is a minimal requirement of a fulfilled life. We also want to thrive and flourish.

Womanist theology understands itself to be a liberation theology. However, liberation appears to be existential more than political. It appears related to the construction of a positive self-consciousness that is fundamentally defined by the heroic qualities of black women's genius (strength and creative resistance against racism, sexism, and classism). Still, the womanist consciousness, proposed in this theology, tends to mirror those qualities of authentic black consciousness that were defined in the revolutionary discourse of the black theology project— a male-dominated discourse that is indebted to European nationalistic impulses and philosophical existentialism for its legitimacy.

The womanist theologian has become, it seems, the mirror of black masculinity: strong and rebellious, surviving and resisting, heroic and epochal. As the mirror of black heroic genius, womanist theology remains devoted to ontological blackness. However, the promise of cultural transcendence proffered by the womanist theologian's self-defining nomenclature, *womanist*, appears subjugated under ontological blackness.

Cheryl J. Sanders (1989), an African American Christian ethicist at Howard University, makes problematic the womanist theologian's ability to transcend the aporias of ontological blackness. In order to suggest how it is an improper basis for constructive womanist theology, Sanders highlights the ways that Alice Walker's construal of a *womanist* transcends ontological blackness by affirming black lesbian love and relativizing race or color. Sanders worries that if Walker's womanist connotations are made regulative in black women's consciousness, the womanist theologian renders herself an alienated theologian, cut off from the *real interests* that structure black life. Therefore, it is possible that the real interests of black life and those of black women's subjectivity can be at odds. Sanders wonders in what sense womanist theology can be womanist, if not all of the connotative marks Walker commends are retrieved by the theologian.

Sanders charges her womanist theological colleagues as having bought into a highly loaded definition of *womanism*. It is a definition that is at its core anti-Christian and anti-black. Womanism is anti-Christian insofar as it is categorically secular. That is, as Sanders see it, womanism is the extention of the modernist moral impulses that are driven by individualism and moral autonomy, and are religiously antinomian. Womanism is antiblack insofar as its openness to homosexual love devalues the real interests of black life, which are the sustaining of black families and the wholeness of the black community.

If I read Sanders's essay correctly, she charges her womanist colleagues with making a categorical error. The error is their identifying the freedoms and transcendence Walker anticipates in her womanist connotations with ontological blackness. "I suspect that it is Christianity and not womanism," Sanders says, "that forms the primary ground of theological and ethical identity with our audacious, serious foremothers" (91).

Sanders understands *womanism* as a secular category that black women theologians have good warrants for rejecting:

> Walker's definition comprises an implicit ethics of moral autonomy, liberation, sexuality and love that is not contingent upon the idea of God or revelation. In any case, to be authentically "womanist" a theological or ethical statement should embrace the full complement of womanist criteria without omissions or additions intended to sanctify, de-

feminize or otherwise alter the perspective Walker intended the word womanist to convey. (87)

According to Sanders, the inclusion of womanism into the construction of black women's theology is defective because black women's experience is categorically based on theistic principles, biblical faith, and a moral tradition that eschews the radical claims to sexual autonomy that Walker commends.

Sanders casts the womanist theological debate in terms of an ontological dilemma. If womanist theologians affirm the privilege of self-definition and the racial and cultural transcendence promised by Walker's womanist connotations, then they risk alienating themselves from the real interests of black life. On the other hand, if they mitigate their claims for womanism, then they risk self-referential inconsistency as womanists. She writes:

> In my view there is a fundamental discrepancy between the womanist criteria that would affirm and/or advocate homosexual practice, and the ethical norms the black church might employ to promote the survival and wholeness of black families. It is problematic for those of us who claim connectedness to and concern for the black family and church to engage these criteria authoritatively and/or uncritically in the formulation of theological-ethical discourse for the two institutions. If black women's ethics is to be pertinent to the needs of our community, then at least some of us must be in a position to offer intellectual guidance to the church as the principal (and perhaps only remaining) advocate for marriage and family in the black community. There is a need for the black churches to promote a positive sexual ethics within the black community as one means of responding to the growing normalization of the single-parent family, and the attendant increases in poverty, welfare dependency, and a host of other problems. (90)

Sanders's internal critique of womanist theology is provocative but flawed on several points. First, Sanders's insistence that in order to qualify as an authentic or *real* womanist, one must buy all of Walker's connotations, begs the question as to whether one might legitimately be resigned to a mitigated version of Walker's womanism. Jacquelyn Grant may well be an instance of a mitigated womanist. Grant's categorical rejection of whiteness does not require that she reject all other connotations of womanism, neither does it prevent her from adding a few other connotations of her own among the existing ones Walker proposes. A mitigated womanism is possible because the various connotations signified by *womanism* are not themselves logically dependent. Therefore, by insisting that womanist consciousness be ultimately bound by Walker's connotations, Sanders mistakes connotative utterances (the meanings of which are extrinsic and conventional) for denotative ones (the meanings of which are intrinsic and essential). In Grant's case, her racial conclusions only make her a mitigated womanist, they do not make her an inconsistent one. Sanders's proposed womanist theological dilemma is unsuccessful.

Second, Sanders would have done better to avoid the argument from secularism in her internal critique of womanist theology. The argument leads her to an untenable disjunction (either/or) between womanism and Christianity. It is clear that for Sanders the word *secular,* in her critique of womanist ethics, is pejorative. *Secular* is used by Sanders to connote a modernist orientation in morals that privileges radical autonomy expressed as the power of self-definition and that ethically affirms monistic forms of spirituality as Walker does. If these characteristics are expressive of womanism's moral and spiritual dispositions, then womanists stand in good company among Christian humanists for whom autonomous moral action is constitutive of the moral life and for whom the unity of all beings coheres in radical monotheistic faith. Such a religious humanism makes possible a *secular* theology. This is a possibility that Sanders's disjunctive opposition between secularism and Christianity does not admit.

Sanders misconstrues the womanist theological debate when she casts it in terms of secularism versus Christianity. Rather, the conflicts are more accurately internal ones among black women who hold incommensurable Christian sensibilities and theologies. That is, the conflict may be between women whose moral and religious sensibilities are commensurable with a secular theology if not a biblical or evangelical one. This point is emphasized in the roundtable responses to Sanders by her womanist colleagues, Cannon, Townes, Copeland, hooks, and Gilkes.

Kelly Brown Douglas casts the debate in its sharpest terms when she suggests that what was missed in the roundtable debate was an opportunity for womanist theologians to make clear their unambiguous no to heterosexism and homophobia in womanist theology (1994, 100–101).

For Sanders, the criteria of legitimacy in African American religion and theology is ontological blackness. And black women theologians' legitimacy is determined by their identifications with black crises. This places black women theologians in a dilemma, according to Sanders. They may choose either the power of self-definition and the actualization of interests that support the celebration of personality and risk alienation from the real interests of black life. Or they may choose to act on the real interests of black life and sacrifice their claims to self-defining personality. In either case, ontological blackness renders black women's consciousness an alienated consciousness. And that is a tragic choice predicated on a false dichotomy between personality and community.

■   ■   ■

Sanders's disjunctive reasoning renders her critique of womanist theology unpersuasive. Nevertheless, her argument crystalizes the problem facing the womanist theological project. Can womanist theology transcend the aporias of ontological blackness and, at the same time, hold to the transcending openings that Walker's womanist connotations commend?

This is not a question peculiar to womanist theology. It is a question posed to other African American theologies where ontological blackness determines the exceptional and existential meanings connected with black life and experience. When black life is fundamentally determined by the totality of a binary racial dialectic that admits no possibility of cultural transcendence, then African American theologians hold few prospects for effectively ameliorating the social and existential crises that bind black life. Talk about liberation becomes hard to justify where freedom appears as nothing more than defiant self-assertion of a revolutionary racial consciousness that requires for its legitimacy the opposition of white racism. Where there exists no possibility of transcending the blackness that whiteness created, African American theologies of liberation must be seen not only as crisis theologies; they remain theologies in a crisis of legitimation.

To press beyond ontological blackness, African American theology needs a public theology that is informed by the enlightening and emancipatory aspects of postmodern African American cultural criticism. It also needs the iconoclastic rigor and utopian dimensions of postmodern African American religious criticism.

four

EXPLICATING AND DISPLACING
ONTOLOGICAL BLACKNESS:

The Heroic and Grotesque
in African American
Cultural and Religious Criticism

■ ■ ■

Chapters 1–3 can be described as provocational for my project in two senses. They anticipate my discourse by calling
me to prior discourses in cultural studies, African American
cultural philosophy, and African American religious thought.
The echoes of these prior discourses are like hearing my
mother shouting from the kitchen and calling me to dinner.
Her voice gets my attention. Second, these prior discourses provoke my discourse. I am not only called to attention by these
other discourses. I also respond. I hear and react to echoes of
prior voices.

Some echoes are more familiar to me than others. Some I
greet with enthusiasm just as I greet an old friend from whom
I have not heard in a long time. A certain nostalgia accompanies
the echoes. Other echoes evoke anxiety, sometimes rage. But
almost always, at least for me, some evoke the nauseous smell
of a high school gym, where one's black masculinity is perform-

atively questioned at the hoops, on the field, at the weights, in the shower, and in signifying on one's mamma.

This discourse on ontological blackness reeks with nostalgia and nausea, familiarity and estrangement, desire and repulsion. Negotiating these ambiguities becomes endlessly burdensome if the only boundaries determining the politics of black identity are structured by binary oppositions that either call for decisive resolutions or do not admit into the dialectical matrices the possibility of cultural transcendence. In aesthetics, African American expressive actions are bound denotatively by the dream of an African American form. In politics, African American leadership is bound by white and black racial ideology, and the politics of exclusion and inclusion they breed. In religion and theology, church and public theologies are determined by white theology and black theology, the righteous oppressed and the damnable oppressors. In these cultural spaces ontological blackness binds all.

In chapters 2 and 3, I explored how ontological blackness contributes to an African American cultural philosophy and theology. In both contexts, black subjectivity is meaningfully related to cultural fulfillment insofar as the various products of African Americans are signs of their cultural genius. I explored the ways that African American identity remains subordinated to the totality of racial ideology and the black heroic genius, and that each is determined by black masculinity. The genius of black masculinity is disclosed in terms of struggle and survival. But in the traditions of the arts, politics, and religion, the fulfillment of black subjectivity, in all its expressive forms, classes, ethnicities, genders, and sexual orientations, takes second seat to racial identity. Blackness is a totality that systematizes African American cultural activities.

In chapter 1, I argued that however we come to understand the concept of religious criticism, it has to be related to culture in two general ways. It must be criticism and it must be religious. In demanding that religious criticism be a function of cultural criticism, it advances both enlightening and culturally emancipatory intentions. And by demanding that it be religious, it examines and promotes ways in which the iconoclastic and edifying intentions of cultural criticism are related to the possibilities of cultural fulfillment. For African Americans, cultural fulfillment has all too often been tied to the ways that African American cultural activities represent the aesthetic genius of the people. But this aesthetic consciousness is also a mirroring of the neoclassicist moral consciousness that was teleologically developed in the European Enlightenment and Romantic heroic self-understanding.

In this last chapter, I critically examine the ways that African American religious criticism can remain a vital source of cultural criticism without basing its self-understanding and legitimacy on ontological blackness and its cult of heroic genius.

EXPLICATING THE HEROIC
AND GROTESQUE GENIUS

In Kant's discourse on the beautiful and sublime, genius is represented in art and music, but particularly in the literature of the people and the laws of nations. It is no coincidence that such an aesthetic consciousness is itself anticipated by the recovery of the Stoic mind in early modern philosophy.

Accompanying this recovery was also a recovery of the heroic epic in European literature. Together, the recovery of the Stoic mind and the retrieval of the heroic epic inaugurated the birth of a neoclassical age, an age that was already anticipated by Machiavelli's classicism but rendered more ethical and more *ingenuous* or noble by Christian ethics. The emergence of this neoclassical age was itself commensurate with the age of Europe and the ethos of north European imperialism. But while the turn to late Greco-Roman antiquities constituted a narrative return, it was not of antiquarian but of ethical interest. The return was itself selective and driven by the newly discovered phenomena of historical consciousness and the possibility of teleological judgment in critical philosophy.

With the emergent age of Europe, European intellectuals understood the dynamics of their times in terms of the epic. The epic is a literary category. It is a complex genre that is wide open to a vast number of developing motifs in literary productions. Such motifs as the heroic person or community, no less than the tragic figure or community, and the comical figure and community, may all be entailed in the epic. The epic may also include within itself effective marks or traits of prior discourses such as lyrical and mythical poetry that speaks to the genius of Greco-Roman antiquities. But it may also anticipate the emergence of new motifs such as the modern novel (Oberhelman, Kelly, and Golsan, 1994, 17). As a marked genre, the epic has an aggrandizing effect on the literary imagination. Characteristic of its internal history and meaning, rather than being episodic, the epic tends to be epochal (17). It is this epochal continuity within the genre that admits its adaptation to motifs that are also narratively or lyrically descriptive of cultural ideologies (Quint, 1993, 15).

It is no surprise that the dominant imperialist ethos and ideology of the age of Europe should have been understood in terms of the epic. In the age of Diderot, Rousseau, Voltaire, and Hume, no less than that of Herder, Goethe, and Coleridge, the literary imagination of European intellectuals was mythically oriented toward the epic. With the recovery of the epic, the heroic also entered the aesthetic consciousness of the times.

The heroic epic contributed to a new humanism in Europe. And the languages of genius, *ingenium, esprit,* and *Geist* inscribed this humanism into the very self-understanding of the eighteenth century. The aesthetic preoccupation of European intellectuals with genius pervades the expressive culture of the times, whether in music, literature, art, philosophy, or theology. The idea of genius has a long career in the West. The idea is based on the Greek word *genea,* which means birth, descent, or race. Its cognates are *genealogia,* which is the tracing of one's pedigree or descent; *genesis* pertains to the origin or to one's birth; *genna* is the generic term for offspring, and *genos* is most philosophically expropriated in metaphysics. It signifies the generality of race, descent, kind, and the general from the species.

In Latin, genius and its cognates begin to have very specialized meanings in relation to culture, places, and times. The Latin idea of genius is derived from the Greek root *gen* but its cognates in Latin are very revealing: *genea* (begotten, production), *genera* (bring forth life), *generosus* (of noble birth), *genesis* (the constellation that presides over one's birth), *genitalis* (belonging to birth, creativity, fruitfulness), *genii* (spirits that guard over one's birth), and *genius* (the guardian spirit of a man or place). English cognates are gene, generic, genre, generation, or general.

The idea of genius in late medieval and early modern thought appears to have emerged with the Florentine renaissance, where the distinction between *ingenium* and *genius* designated the opposition between innate capabilities or powers that are spontaneous and talents or skills that can be acquired by teaching and practice. The idea of genius in art, for instance, tends to be associated with the category of *invention* in rhetoric and poetics. But invention is distinguishable from mimesis or imitation. Already by the mid-sixteenth century, the idea of genius expands from the matrix of art to include science as well. And by the end of the eighteenth century, the idea is used to designate the spirit of an age.

Evident in the history of the idea of genius is that the idea itself achieves a dialectical standing in relation to any number of other aesthetic categories: genius versus talent, genius versus taste, genius versus imitation. But the dialectics of genius comes to signify the opposition of originality, individuality, invention, inspiration, creativity in art, music, philosophy, and politics over tradition, gilded arts, mimesis, discovery, talent, and taste. It must be pointed out that the philosophical problem of genius is its unification with other faculties that constitute the human subject.

For Kant, the integration of genius and taste is to be achieved in a general theory of representational epistemology, says Tonelli:

> He distinguished genius from skill or talent, when these are not creative; genius is opposed to diligence, but needs instruction, and is a favorable proportion of four powers: sensibility, judgement, creative spirit, and taste. Its realm is the production of new ideas and ideals. Genius, freedom, and living organisms are elements which cannot be explained mechanically. (Tonelli, 1973, 295–96)

It was with Herder and the inauguration of the Sturm und Drang movement that the idea of genius achieved cultic proportions and became consistently identified with *Zeitgeist,* or the spirit of the age (although as we saw in Kant's *Beautiful and Sublime,* the idea had already been used by Hume as a term of cultural differentiation).

The French Revolution and the rise of Napoleon rendered the idea of nationalistic or cultural genius no longer an abstraction. It became embodied not only in the figure of Napoleon, but also in an empire, France. Genius signified the European nationalist impulses that would stress nation over individuality, totality over infinity, concretion over abstraction, and the age of Europe over Orientalism (see Said, 1979). The idea of Europe was now justified under the cult of heroic genius in art, music, literature, religion, philosophy, politics, and law.

Ernst Cassirer concludes his momentous essay on *The Philosophy of the Enlightenment* with "The Fundamental Problem of Aesthetics." It is a problem of the Enlightenment's coming to terms with aesthetics' independence from the rule of reason and the project of critical, systematic philosophy. Yet in Lessing, Cassirer sees the unity of aesthetics and critical philosophy consummated:

It is above all because of him that the century of the Enlightenment, to a very great extent dominated by its gift of criticism, did not fall prey to the merely negative critical
function—that it was able to reconvert criticism to creativity
and shape it and use it as an indispensable instrument of
life and of the constant renewal of the spirit. (1951, 360)

In the same tones with which Goethe speaks of Herder as
one who "concentrates with all his might on the factual, the
unique, and the particular without succumbing to the sheer
material power of the factual, to mere 'matter of fact'" and as
one who could "transform the rubbish of history into a living
plant," Cassirer regards Lessing as possessing not only a magic
power in the realm of poetry, but "in the whole realm of eighteenth century philosophy" (359–60). In philosophy, Cassirer
sees Lessing as an exemplary genius:

> Lessing leads the aesthetics of the Enlightenment beyond
> previous goals and frontiers, even though he seems merely
> to inherit its intellectual possessions. He alone was able to
> accomplish what Gottsched and the Swiss critics, Voltaire
> and Diderot, and Shaftesbury and his followers, could not
> achieve. He not only brings the aesthetic thought of an ep-
> och to its climax but, reaching beyond all given realities of
> art, he discovers new possibilities for poetry. His chief merit
> in German literature lies in the fact that he saw the place
> for possibilities and cleared the way for them. This merit is
> vastly underestimated and deprived of its real meaning in
> intellectual history if . . . one finds in his criticism only a
> national, not a European achievement. (359)

To reiterate, the idea of genius profoundly effected the self-
understanding of the age of Europe. The idea was concretized
in the possibility of teleological judgments in history, Hegel's
consummate religion, the development of national literatures,
which created possibilities for comparative literature, constitu-

tional nation-states, and a Eurocentric philosophy of culture. In all these realms of culture, the idea of genius proved to be culturally formative and expressive. Although the cult of genius had a pervasive influence on the cultural philosophy of Europe in the eighteenth and nineteenth centuries, its influence was not total. The nationalistic impulses that it justified faced a counter-discourse on individualism in art and music, and an aesthetic reversal of the heroic epic by tragedy and the grotesque. No figure better crystalized this reversal than Friedrich Nietzsche.

Fundamental to Nietzsche's aesthetical critique of culture is a certain reversal of the Socratic problematic that permeates Plato's dialogues. Is justice finally reducible to the advantage of the strongest or powerful over the weakest? Has Thrasymachus, who argues "that justice is nothing other than the advantage of the stronger," triumphed over Socrates (*Republic*, bk. 1:340b, 1991, 17)? Are Socrates's sparring partners more right than Socrates or the Platonic academy? Nietzsche thinks that such questions were not taken seriously in the history of philosophy. Had they been taken seriously, they would have made a difference to the future of critical philosophy and hence of cultural criticism. So-called critical philosophy continues the separation of speech (i.e., *logos*) from the masks or the persona of Socrates, and from the dramatic qualities of the dialogue. And the idiot, the tragic, the comedic, and the ironic (all the things that best disclose Socrates's character as well as his voice) remain concealed under the dogmatic sincerity of philosophy and subsequently of theology.

> With Socrates Greek taste undergoes a change in favor of dialectics: what is really happening when that happens? It is above all the defeat of a nobler taste; with dialectics the rabble get on top. Before Socrates, the dialectical manner was repudiated in good society; it was regarded as a form of bad manners, one was compromised by it. Young people were warned against it. And all such presentations of one's

reasons was regarded with mistrust. Honest things, like honest men, do not carry their reasons exposed in this fashion. It is indecent to display all one's goods. What has first to have itself proved is of little value. Wherever authority is still part of accepted usage and one does not "give reasons" but commands, the dialectician is a kind of buffoon; he is laughed at, he is not taken seriously—Socrates was the buffoon who got himself taken seriously: what was really happening when that happened? (1990, 41)

By resolving the tensions between justice and power in morality, philosophy foreclosed on its capacity to carry out the demands of critical philosophy. Rather, the unresolvable decay of prior moralities was resolved in the heroic genius. And an Apollonian aesthetic displaced the Dionysian.

This aesthetic dialectic is crucial for recognizing the sort of reversals Nietzsche attempts in his own aesthetic critique of culture. In an important paragraph, Nietzsche explicates the difference.

What is the meaning of the antithetical concepts Apollonian and Dionysian, both conceived as forms of intoxication, which I introduced into aesthetics?—Apollonian intoxication alerts above all the eye, so that it acquires power of vision. The painter, the sculptor, the epic poet are visionaries par excellence. In the Dionysian state, on the other hand, the entire emotional system is alerted and intensified; so that it discharges all its powers of representation, imitation, transfiguration, transmutation, every kind of mimicry and play-acting, conjointly. The essential thing remains the facility of metamorphoses. (84)

Nietzsche's Dionysian aesthetics privileges the grotesque genius over the heroic genius. So it is clear that genius is not at stake in Nietzsche's discourse. We have already seen how prior to Nietzsche the contrast in aesthetic theory was between the heroic and creative genius over taste, imitation, and talent. Where heroic and creative genius signals spontaneity, irreproducibility, and nobility of origin, the Dionysian signals for Nietzsche the grotesque genius:

> It is impossible for the Dionysian man not to understand any suggestion of whatever kind, he ignores no signal from the emotions, he possesses to the highest degree the instinct for understanding and divining, just as he possesses the art of communication to the highest degree. He enters into every skin, into every emotion; he is continually transforming himself. (84)

The grotesque genius, like the heroic, is fundamentally an aesthetic conception. Nietzsche does not invent the grotesque. For like the heroic, the grotesque too has had a long career—albeit a rather repressed one. According to Philip Thomson:

> The grotesque is not of course a phenomenon solely of the twentieth century, not even of modern civilization. It existed as an artistic mode in the West at least as far back as the early Christian period of Roman culture, where there evolved a style of combining human, animal and vegetable elements, intricately interwoven, in the one painting. (1972, 12)

This short note from Thomson's book introduces constitutive elements that identify the grotesque. The grotesque ought not to be thought of as an opposition between two diametrically opposed sensibilities such as would occur in binary dialectics. Yet the grotesque does have to do with sensibilities that are oppositional, such as attraction and repulsion, and pleasure and pain differentials. However, the grotesque seeks neither negation nor mediation between these sensibilities. Rather, it leaves them in tension, unresolved by negation or mediation. Thomson describes the grotesque thus:

The most consistently distinguished characteristic of the grotesque has been the fundamental element of disharmony, whether this is referred to as conflict, clash, mixture of the heterogeneous, or conflation of disparates. It is important that this disharmony has been seen, not merely in the work of art as such, but also in the reaction it produces and (speculatively) in the creative temperament and psychological make-up of the artist. (20)

While Thomson captures certain essential marks of the grotesque, the disharmonious quality of the grotesque requires further explication. The disharmony of the grotesque may be compared to that of an optical game, such as "Duck or Rabbit," "Man's Face or Nude," or the infamous "Wife or Mother-in-Law" drawings. Each drawing shares elements of the grotesque, which Frederick Burwick recognizes in many literary classics identified as grotesques. Burwick is worth quoting at length because his description of the grotesque will be illustrative for claims I want to press for the grotesque:

Certainly, one of the major functions of the grotesque is to give us the illusion of delusion. Genius deliberately assumes the pretensions of madness to exhibit the unfettered fecundity of the imagination. This is why delusion is frequently thematized in grotesque literature and art. In order to create grotesque illusion, the artist turns to delusion for his subject-matter. What we often find in these paintings is the portrait of someone having a delusion complete with a depiction of the delusion. Among the most often cited examples of the grotesque are the many versions—Grunewald, Bosch, Callot—of the Temptation of Saint Anthony. Or, for literary examples, one might cite such tales as Hoffmann's *The Sandman*, Poe's *The Tell-Tale Heart*, Kafka's *Metamorphosis*, Browning's *Madhouse Cells*, told by a narrative persona who is deranged, whose view of the world is tinged with madness. It is not the content, per se, that renders these works grotesque; rather, it is the peculiar tension of dual perception which is required in responding to the grotesque. We must experience the work as illusion yet recognize it as delusion. The grotesque, then, involves an elaborate multistability of manner and matter. This was Friedrich Schlegel's reason for defining the grotesque as a mode of irony, for he recognized in the grotesque a challenge to the mind's instinctive endeavor to synthesize. (Burwick, 1990, 129–30)

Several important features of Burwick's analysis provoke claims I want to make for the grotesque—albeit from the side of British aesthetic theory. First, the grotesque recovers and leaves unresolved prior and basic sensibilities such as attraction/repulsion and pleasure/pain differentials, each of which formed the basis of British aesthetic theory (such as Shaftesbury's) and Lockean epistemology (which is also predicated on perception and apperception of cognitive matrices). Second, the nonresolution of these aesthetic and cognitive matrices renders the objects perceived and our apperception of the object confused or ambiguous. Third, these unresolved tensions may leave possibilities open for creative ways of taking an object or subject; for in the grotesque, an object is, at the same time, other than how it appears when one contour or another is attenuated. Fourth, the grotesque disrupts the penchant for cognitive synthesis and the aggrandizing functions of cultural genius and the heroic epic by highlighting the absurd and sincere, the comical and tragic, the estranged and familiar, the satirical and the playful, and normalcy and abnormalcy (Thomson, 1972, 20–57).

To return to Nietzsche's aesthetic critique of culture, the dissonance that characterizes the grotesque is more like the tensions that occur not so much as in the *play of music* but in the tuning of the strings by the tuning fork. Perhaps no passage speaks as pointedly to this image as Nietzsche's foreword to *Twilight of the Idols:*

To stay cheerful when involved in a gloomy and exceedingly responsible business is no inconsiderable art: yet what could be more necessary than cheerfulness? Nothing succeeds in which high spirits play no part. Only excess of strength is proof of strength.—*A revaluation of values*, this question mark so black, so huge it casts a shadow over him who sets it up—such a destiny of a task compels one every instant to run out into the sunshine so as to shake off a seriousness grown all too oppressive. . . . A maxim whose origin I withhold from learned curiosity has long been my motto: "The spirit grows, Strength is restored by wounding." . . . Another form of recovery, in certain cases even more suited to me, is to sound out idols. . . . This little book is a *grand declaration of war*; and as regards the sounding-out of idols, this time they are not idols of the age but eternal idols which are here touched with the hammer as with a tuning fork. (1990, 31–32)

Nietzsche's aesthetical critique of culture must be understood as an instance of imminent criticism. The specter of the heroic and the burden of cultural genius are always present. As Nietzsche says in *The Gay Science*, "God is dead; but given the ways of men, there may still be caves for thousands of years in which his shadow will be shown—And we—we still have to vanquish his shadow too" (1974, bk. 3, par:108, 167). The seriousness of metaphysics and theology is often resolved in cynicism when genius is unfulfilled, or in extravagant optimism when genius discloses itself in the cultural products of a national music or literature.

In turning to the Dionysian aesthetic, which is at the same time a turn to the grotesque, Nietzsche regards pessimism as worthy, while making gaiety and laughter its corollary. He thought of his own contribution to the critique of culture, *The Birth of Tragedy* (1956), as advancing:

A pessimism situated "beyond good and evil;" a perversity of stance of the kind Schopenhauer spent all his life fulminating against; a philosophy which dared place ethics among the phenomena (and so "demote" it)—or rather, place it not even among phenomena in the idealistic sense but among the "deceptions." (10)

The critic's stance is not only that of a hearty *pessimism,* but pessimism remains in creative tension with *laughter.* Echoing Zarathustra, Nietzsche's intention in criticism is to teach one to laugh while at the same time admonishing the disposition of pessimism:

> I would rather have you learn, first, the art of terrestrial comfort; teach you how to laugh—if that is, you really insist on remaining pessimists. And then it may perhaps happen that one fine day you will, with a peal of laughter, send all metaphysical palliatives packing, metaphysics herself leading the great exodus. (14–15)

In Nietzsche's discourse, the grotesque genius displaces but does not negate the heroic, Apollonian genius and the seriousness of morals it breeds. For Nietzsche, the grotesque must open up creative possibilities for a Dionysian genius if critical philosophy is to fulfill its iconoclastic and creative intentions. The grotesque requires a transvaluation of values whereby the heroic qualities of the Apollonian cult of genius are reoccupied in the grotesque. Nietzsche asks, "What makes a hero?" His answer is: "Going out to meet at the same time one's highest suffering and one's highest hope" (*The Gay Science,* bk. 3, par: 268, 1974, 219).

The Birth of Tragedy puts forward a counter-discourse to that generated by the aesthetic preoccupation with the epic. In that text, Nietzsche anticipates the question that now locates my own interest in aesthetic and moral philosophy when he asks, "What should a music look like which is no longer romantic in inspiration, like the German, but Dionysian instead?" (13). I ask myself, in this book, what should African American cultural and religious criticism look like when they are no longer romantic in inspiration and the cult of heroic genius is displaced by the grotesquery of contemporary black expressive culture and public life? I turn to these questions in the next two sections.

NEW LITERARY CRITIQUES OF
AFRICAN AMERICAN EXPRESSIVE CULTURE

African American cultural philosophy owes a debt to European aesthetics. To be sure, there were profound circumstances that occasioned its development. Racial ideology was dependent on categorical racism: people of African descent were regarded as belonging to a separate species, one that was not quite human in intelligence, understanding, or cultural consciousness, and exhibited no cultural genius. African Americans defined themselves also in terms of categorical racism. Their expressive culture achieved legitimacy as it reflected the genius of the people. Advancing the heroic qualities of black culture became both the motive and end of black subjectivity.

The meaning of black subjectivity was based on culture and was determined by the totality of race in a double sense. First, within this aesthetic matrix black racial identity was answerable to the exclusionary politics of white racism. Second, loyalty to racial identity also provided a matrix of social acceptability within the black community. Therefore, racial devotion provided insider-outsider possibilities in the black community itself. But there is a need to go beyond this cult of black heroic genius, particularly if black subjectivity is to actualize itself in the context of postmodern North American culture.

African American literary criticism points beyond ontological blackness and its cult of black heroic genius to the grotesquery of postmodern blackness. Henry Lewis Gates, Jr., recognizes that racial apologetic interests have for the most part determined African American cultural philosophy and expressive culture. But he also recognizes the ambiguities entailed in the notion of black aesthetics. Gates poses the classical ambiguity in terms of whether "black poetry is racial in theme or [whether] black poetry [is] any sort of poetry written by black people?" (1992, 26). Gates argues that the traditional answer tends to fall on the first pole. And quoting James Weldon Johnson, Gates writes:

> No people that has produced great literature and art has ever been looked upon by the world as distinctly inferior. The status of the Negro in the United States is more a question of national mental attitude toward the race than of actual conditions. And nothing will do more to change that mental attitude and raise his status than a demonstration of intellectual parity by the Negro through the production of literature and art. (26)

Drawing attention to the racial aesthetic and the African American canon of Calverton at the end of the Harlem renaissance, Gates summarizes its meaning as "a canon that was unified thematically by self-defense against racist literary conventions, and by the expression of what the editors called 'strokes of freedom'" (29).

When Gates examines the reception of the racial aesthetics in the canon formed by Amiri Baraka and Larry Neal, in their *Black Fire* (1968), he criticizes it as signaling no significant movement from the prior experiments in canon formation grounded in racial apologetics. In this anthology, Gates sees one essential model replaced by another essential model. Indeed, it is "the blackest canon of all" (30). He writes:

> The hero, the valorized presence in this volume is the black vernacular: no longer summoned or invoked through familiar and comfortable rubrics such as "The Spirituals" and "The Blues," but *embodied, assumed, presupposed* in a marvelous act of formal bonding often obscured by the stridency of the political message the anthology meant to announce.

Absent completely was a desire to "prove" our common humanity with white people, by demonstrating our power of intellect. One mode of essentialism—"African" essentialism—was used to critique the essentialism implicit in notions of a common or universal American heritage. NO, in *Black Fire,* art and act were one. (31)

For Gates, if the classical black aesthetics sought to disclose black expressive genius in terms of racial consciousness, it did so only by negating black subjectivity and constructing an essentialist litmus test. The multifaceted aspects of African American vernacular collapsed under the totality of black power and black genius. African American subjects remained alienated from their products.

Writing some fifty years after James Weldon Johnson, Albert Murray seeks to reassure the classical black aesthetics in African American expressive culture when he writes:

The creation of an art style is, as most anthropologists would no doubt agree, a major cultural achievement. In fact, it is perhaps the highest as well as the most comprehensive fulfillment of culture; for an art style, after all, reflects nothing so much as the ultimate synthesis and refinement of a life style.

Art is by definition a process of stylization; and what it stylizes is experience. What it objectifies, embodies, abstracts, expresses, and symbolizes is a sense of life. Accordingly, what is represented in the music, dance, painting, sculpture, literature, and architecture, of a given group of people in a particular time, place, and circumstance is a conception of the essential nature and purpose of human existence itself. More specifically, an art style is the assimilation in terms of which a given community, folk, or communion of faith embodies its basic attitudes toward experience. (1970, 54–55)

Murray connects the nineteenth century symbolic, expressive aesthetics to black cultural productions in ways that reassure the viability of the classical black aesthetics. In its application to African American cultural production, the *essential meaning* of the productions are rendered just so much "survival techniques" and "the need to live in style" (55).

The classical black aesthetic construes African American expressive culture as a stylization of "the struggles for political and social liberty" and "a quest for freedom to choose one's own way or style of life" (56). But expressing one's style of life, Murray suggests, ought not to be thought of in terms of a purely voluntary subjectivity. Rather, he says, "it should be equally as obvious that there can be no such thing as human dignity and nobility without a consummate definitive style, pattern, or archetypal image" (56): an African American form. In Murray's aesthetic judgment, the blues is the representational form of black cultural genius:

> The blues ballad is a good example of what the blues are about. Almost always relating a story of frustration, it could hardly be described as a device for avoiding the unpleasant facts of Negro life in America. On the contrary, it is a very specific and highly effective vehicle, the obvious purpose of which is to make Negroes acknowledge the essentially tenuous nature of human existence. (57)

In *Blues, Ideology, and African American Literary Criticism* (1984), Houston Baker, Jr., attempts to take seriously the notion that African American culture must somehow be analyzed in terms of expressive form(s). With Murray, he sees the blues as good a candidate as any other form. Yet he also proposes to decenter the cultural aesthetic theory that links critics of African expressive culture from James Weldon Johnson to Albert Murray—namely, the quest for a definitive form.

Rather than seeing the blues as a categorical structure of meaning (108), Baker sees the blues as tropological. It is expressive of the improvocational ways that blacks give meaning to their experiences of America. But as a tropological signifier, the blues not only bears the marks of travel narratives governed by self-reflection on black experience. The blues is also a self-reflexive discourse:

> In my study as a whole, I attempt persuasively to demonstrate that a blues matrix (as a vernacular trope for American cultural explanation in general) possesses enormous force for the study of literature, criticism, and culture. I know that I have appropriated the vastness of the vernacular in the United States to a single matrix. But I trust that my necessary selectivity will be interpreted, not as a sign of myopic exclusiveness, but as an invitation to inventive play. The success of my efforts would be effectively signaled . . . . by the transformation of my "I" into a juncture where readers could freely improvise their own distinctive tropes for cultural explanation. (1984, 14)

Baker is keenly aware that the turn to vernacular analysis will not guarantee a definitive expressive form structured around essential qualities. Elsewhere Baker argues that critics' failure to adequately distinguish connotative utterances from denotative ones often leads to consequences that disrupt effective criticism. When African American critics mistake denotative utterances (those utterances that function in the indicative mode and imply what is the case) for what are really connotative utterances (those utterances that signify the extrinsic qualities of an object or activity), then the critic renders multivalent qualities of expressive cultural production essential (1980, 132–54). While expressive of the historical determinants of the economy of slavery, the blues is also expressive of black subjectivity, and such expressions do not always support the essentialized claims made by the black aesthetic school. The blues as self-reflexive discourse may decenter the prospects for an African American form because it is expressive of styles of life that valorize misogyny, adultery, drunken resolve, and moral failures that other valorizations of the blues may tend to conceal. Baker accents the grotesque quality of the blues in his attempt to free up African American cultural criticism from the aporias of essentialized black aesthetics.

Other critics, such as Toni Morrison, Madhu Dubey, bell hooks, and Joe Wood, also call into question the totalizing frames under which the classical black aesthetic distorts the thick, rich complexities that characterize African American cultural practices. Yet their challenges are confined to a rather isolated discourse in American universities and colleges. Nevertheless, the insights gained from both literary and philosophical criticism in African American cultural studies of the past two decades make it increasingly difficult to maintain the viability of the classical black aesthetic and its application in cultural criticism.

In her critical essays, Morrison explains her writing projects as exercises in self-reflexive formations of consciousness in expressive productions:

> Writing and reading are not all that distinct for a writer. Both exercises require being alert and ready for unaccountable beauty, for intricateness or simple elegance of the writer's imagination, for the world that imagination evokes. Both require being mindful of the places where imagination sabotages itself, locks its own gates, pollutes its vision. Writing and reading mean being aware of the writer's notions of risk and safety, the serene achievement of, or sweaty fight for, meaning and response-ability. (1992, xi)

Morrison attempts to displace the emphasis on racial representation not only in the American literary canon but also in African American literary productions. She attends to what is called racing. Race is an inevitable category of reading and writing in American expressive culture (11). Morrison is interested in neither justifying nor ignoring race/racing, nor is she interested in totalizing it in her writings. Rather, in some very telling remarks, she eloquently describes the self-reflexive intentions of racing in the new literary critique of African American cultural philosophy. She writes: "My project is an effort to avert the critical gaze from the racial object to the racial subject; from the described and imagined to the describers and imaginers; from the serving to the served" (90).

In demanding that literary criticism be self-reflexive in intention, Morrison displaces those modes of writing and reading that turn on self-reflective consciousness and bind discourse between subject/object, white/black, innocence/guilt, victim/victimizers, and virtuous/perverse dialectics, which circumscribe African presence in American literature. "The kind of work I have always wanted to do," Morrison states, "requires me to learn how to maneuver ways to free up the language from its sometimes sinister, frequently lazy, almost always predictable employment of racially informed and determined chains" (xi).

Madhu Dubey persuasively locates the uses of the classical black aesthetic in the cultural nationalist movement of the sixties and early seventies. She also provides a persuasive account of its dead ends as cultural criticism in a context that has now come to exonerate difference:

The contemporary black feminist discourse on identity is motivated by an impulse to displace the prescriptive model of black identity, unified around the sign of race, that was promoted by Black Aesthetic critics. Along with Deborah McDowell, black feminist theorists such as Hortense Spillers and Karla Halloway are insistently foregrounding the "convergences of difference," the "spaces of contradiction," the "polysemic ramifications of fracture," and the "persistence of the decentered subject" in black women's fiction. Emphasizing the multiple orders of difference that constitute the black feminine subject, these theorists seek to resist the totalizing moves of other discourses on the subject, such as the definition of "man" in bourgeois humanist ideology, of "woman" in white feminist ideology, and of "black" in black nationalist ideology. In the early black feminist discourse on images of black women in literature, the term *black woman* tends to congeal into a stable and given category. It is precisely this "critical tendency to homogenize and essentialize black women" that is interrogated in the writings of contemporary black feminist critics such as McDowell, Spillers, and Holloway. (1994, 3)

Critics like Morrison and Dubey attempt to displace the classical black aesthetic by accenting grotesque characters who disclose the often less than *moral manliness* representational of black genius (Dubey, 1994, 33–35). Commenting on Morrison's *The Bluest Eye*, Dubey writes: "The novel's presentation of rape, incest, and madness flagrantly flouts the black nationalist injunction that black art 'must divorce itself from the sociological attempt to explain the black community in terms of pathology'" (33). But the form of criticism that Morrison and Dubey exercise in their attempts to reveal the real and unauthentic interests of the individuated subject ought not to be seen as an outright rejection of the heroic qualities of black life which the black aesthetics seeks to reassure. Dubey comments on and cites Morrison: "Morrison's conception of her work also confirms the black aesthetic belief that art should be political and should address the black community: 'if anything I do . . . isn't about the village or the community or about you, then it is not about anything . . . which is to say, yes, the work must be political'" (1994, 34).

Morrison and Dubey displace the black heroic genius by foregrounding the morally, racially, and spiritually ambiguous actions of blacks and black communities in their critiques of black life and communities. Yet the new literary critique of African American cultural philosophy is inescapably political. Again, quoting Morrison, Dubey writes: "The novel should be beautiful and powerful, but it should work. It should have something that enlightens; something in it that opens the door and points the way" (Dubey, 1994, 34; compare Morrison, 1984). Insofar as the new literary criticism intends both enlightenment and emancipation, it is a vital source for African American cultural and religious criticism.

Perhaps one of the most provocative advocates of a new black aesthetic in African American religious and cultural criticism is bell hooks. With rigor, hooks attempts to get past the cult of black heroic genius (1981, 1990, and 1991). She asks a question both provocative and explosive: "How do we create an oppositional world view, a consciousness, an identity, a standpoint that exists not only as that struggle which also opposes dehumanization but as that movement which enables creative, expansive self-actualization?" (1990, 15). hooks argues that the classical aesthetics eclipsed black women's difference under a cult of racial ideology and black moral manliness (the latter quite literally). Black classical aesthetics also perpetuates the Western, imperial practices that define the very society that black leaders, liberal and radical, sought to dismantle. And the culture of black politics and religious criticism, she argues, totalized black women's subjectivity under a black essentialism.

hooks envisions a form of cultural criticism that defies the perpetuation of white colonization under black liberation masks that themselves "[insist] on patriarchal values, on equating black liberation with black men gaining access to male privilege that would enable them to assert power over black women" (16). Conversely, hooks proposes that "a visible split has emerged between many black men and women, one that suggests our concerns are not similar, that we do not share a common ground where we can engage in critical dialogue about aesthetics, gender, feminist politics, etc." (17).

hooks is not suggesting that there are no solidarities among African Americans who seek to engage critically the meaning of black subjectivity. Rather, the solidarity that hooks envisions among African American critics is one that acknowledges that black subjectivity is bound not only by racist structuralism, but also by sexist, heterosexist, and class totalities as well. Of the company of cultural critics who propose a new black aesthetics, hooks writes:

> We are avant-garde only to the extent that we eschew essen-
> tialist notions, epistemologies, habits of being, concrete class
> locations, and radical political commitments. We believe in
> solidarity and are working to make spaces where black
> women and men can dialogue about everything, spaces
> where we can engage in critical dissent without violating
> one another. We are concerned with black culture and black
> identity. (19)

This turn among African American cultural critics to a new black aesthetic is eloquently inscribed in what Joe Wood calls, "The New Blackness:"

> We take our humanity for granted, and we realize that our
> community is made up of people of all sorts of colors, gen-
> ders, classes, ethnicities, sexuality, etc. . . . . "Race" is a dying
> category; Whiteness, and the Blackness it makes for itself,
> is dying too. We will seize the day and make a new Blackness.
>   Our new Blackness acknowledges the way each of us live
> beyond the Black community. I am a multitude of names,
> masks, community memberships. Denying this is tyranny—
> "race" is not my only state. . . . I make new communities all
> the time. Which does not make me a "multiculturalist" or
> a "cultural Mulatto"—it makes me a human being in the
> world. . . . I am about making Blackness—the next step is
> to create a new and compelling politics to push the discourse
> forward. We talk. (1992, 15–16)

Wood's manifesto names the substantive goods that are predicated on difference. What makes Wood's manifesto a persuasive
instance of cultural criticism is not only the utopian connotations it commends, but also the iconoclastic aspects of religious
criticism at work in his criticism. Wood names and exposes the

conditions under which African American life and experience are conducted. Black life is fundamentally structured by differences that mitigate any totalized discourse on racial aesthetics or essentialized *racing* of African American presence in American cultural production.

The new literary critiques of African American cultural philosophy are not naive about the pervasive and historic influences of white racial ideology on the construction of black presence and identity. However, any failure to acknowledge the effects of racism/racing in the politics of black identity must render talk about constructing a new politics of difference internally incoherent. For it is very difficult to explicate connotatively the *new* without at the same time displacing those prior discourses that have representationally structured African American cultural life.

What makes the new literary critiques of African American cultural philosophy new is the centrality of the grotesque in cultural analysis. The grotesque highlights the morally ambiguous African American presence in American life. It is oriented toward the ways that black life is an unresolved confusion of the frivolous and serious, the morally virtuous and perverse, the historical but often episodic, and the empty and fulfilled. The new literary critiques of African American cultural philosophy renders the grotesque heroic, and the critic is freed up to play in the unresolved ambiguities of black life. The new literary critics of African American cultural philosophy advance a conception of cultural criticism that is at once iconoclastic and utopian.

THE GROTESQUERY OF AFRICAN AMERICAN PUBLIC LIFE

The form of African American religious criticism that I commend does not regard culture as ultimate or total. Rather, the task of religious criticism is to expose the forgotten memory among African Americans that all cultures, including our own, are human artifacts. Exposing such a memory lies at the heart of my cultural and religious critique of ontological blackness. The aesthetic critique of culture does not only displace the heroic by the grotesque, it also opens up new possibilities for how African Americans can *take each other* in public life with aesthetic sensibilities that resist eclipsing individuality under collectivity. Both aspects of identity formation have to find a place in the new cultural politics of difference, if it is not merely to mirror the dead ends of the classical black aesthetics, its cult of black heroic genius, and its totalization in ontological blackness.

In an important essay, bell hooks recounts the functions of the classical black aesthetics in public life and its radicalization in the 1960s and 70s. She writes:

> Whatever African-Americans created in music, dance, poetry, painting, etc., it was regarded as testimony, bearing witness, challenging racist thinking which suggested that black folks were not fully human, were uncivilized, and that the measure of this was our collective failure to create "great" art. White supremacist ideology insisted that black people, being more animal than human, lacked the capacity to feel and therefore could not engage the finer sensibilities that were the breeding ground for art. Responding to this propaganda, nineteenth-century black folks emphasized the importance of art and cultural production, seeing it as the most effective challenge to such assertions. (1990, 105)

hook's historical note captures many of the claims that I make for the functions of the classical black aesthetics. The central claim is that the aesthetic theory and practices of African Americans were, and to a great extent still are, bound by white racial ideology and the cult of black heroic genius. I am not interested in either commending or assigning culpability to these past projects in African American cultural criticism. I am not saying that the cultural nationalism of the 1960s and early

70s and its influence on African American aesthetics is blame-worthy for its identification of black aesthetics with "revolution-ary politics" (106). What I stress are certain consequences of this aesthetic for the subsequent development of African American cultural philosophy under today's drastically changed condi-tions in which neither the protest politics of the 1960s nor the revolutionary rhetoric of the 70s seem effective.

I share with hooks deep suspicion about the ways that this racial aesthetic conceals levels of cultural differentiation among African Americans. My accents on difference have the quality of an emphatic utterance that is punctuated by multiple excla-mations: *Difference!!!!!* By emphasizing that the discourse on difference that I propose is a highly nuanced one, I do not wish to deprive those cultural philosophies that prize racial and even gender difference of their urgently needed provocations. Rather, my intention is to alert critics of the linguistic dangers of reifying the categories that govern their discourses in such a way as to mimic, represent, and mirror the discourses they want to reject. I agree with hooks that "a retrospective examina-tion of the repressive impact a prescriptive black aesthetic had on black cultural production should serve as a cautionary model for African-Americans" (111). Such a cautionary note should also extend to the critique of African American theology.

Chapter 3 discussed the ways that African American religious thinkers lend their loyalties to the legitimation of ontological blackness by advancing black identity in terms of black mascu-linity, moral manliness, heroic discontent, and racial self-definition. African American theologians' support of black reli-gious experience, as survival, resistance, and revolutionary, ap-proaches mythical proportions.

In a much neglected essay, Adolph L. Reed tries to correct what he sees as an *exaggerated, heroic,* and *histrionic* account of the churches' claims to moral primacy and civic leadership in black protest politics (1986, 45, 51, 57). He emphasizes the less than avant-garde ways that the black churches and their reli-gious leaders interacted with the protest politics of the civil rights era. He also highlights the place of the churches as organizational sites in the mobilization of black interests in politics. But the interests themselves, he argues, were not raised to public consciousness by the black churches (48).

Rather, the black churches and their religious leaders tended to provide a structure of legitimization for black politics. However, they themselves tended not to be strategically interventionists in protest activism. "A more accurate representation," Reed argues, "locates the church's role in protest politics mainly in provision of institutional support for activities initiated and led under other auspices" (51). Such auspices have been student movements, the NAACP, and other nonreligious based grassroots protest organizations and coalitions, many of which were directed by the activity of professionals (teachers, lawyers, and the business class) and their respective interests.

Reed's argument demonstrates the ways that social and political differentiation (particularly the one between the clerical elite class and the electorial elite class) call into question any uncritical acceptance of the Apollonian myth of the black churches. Whether the black churches and their clerical elites are viable contenders for the moral and political loyalties of African Americans today remains a question open for religious criticism. However, religious criticism cannot foreclose on answering this question affirmatively from the start. It is possible that with a generation of clergy and laity educated in liberal arts and social and cultural criticism, there may be resurgent possibilities for an effective critique of culture from the side of the churches and their leaders. However, such a possibility will call for a form of religious criticism that can articulate the real interests of African Americans in the realm of public opinion. And the realm of public opinion is where they are most likely to be politically influential (West, 1988, 273–80).

My proposal for African American religious criticism is dispositionally grotesque. But I also recognize that there are limits to aesthetic critiques of culture. Religious criticism must be both enlightening and emancipatory in its normative and descriptive functions. This requires critiques of ideology that are not only descriptive and pejorative but also positive. This means that the religious critic cannot be content with a self-imposed ascetical detachment from the work of actualizing the demands of a new politics of difference: there remains the structural transformation of the public sphere.

The positive critique of ideology engages the critics' capacities to construct counter-worldviews and advocate alternative or corrective moral visions. To be sure, in religious and cultural criticism, both social and cultural analyses are pertinent. But questions such as—what is to be done? and what conditions are necessary for action?—are also relevant, particularly if the governing category of fulfillment is to orient religious and cultural criticism. The internal dynamics of African American religious criticism do not only call for social, cultural, religious, and philosophical analyses, but if religious criticism is in the service of a new politics of difference, it must also place itself at risk in the public realm. And the public realm that African American critics inhabit is fraught with fragility, social differentiation along class, gender, racial/ethnic, sexual interests, and the threat of urban nihilism in African American youth culture (West, 1993, 11ff.).

The public realm that African American religious critics want to influence poses considerable difficulties. The public spaces that critics hope to influence are greatly differentiated. African American critics are judged relevant in that realm more or less by how they construe community and personality in relation to racialized culture. Critics are judged relevant in terms of race loyalty and racial authenticity, says Michael Dyson:

> Taken together, these rhetorics compose the moral center of a politics of racial propriety, used by some black intellectuals to determine what is legitimate and acceptable for a widening body of black cultural expression. Loyalty to race has been historically construed as primary and unquestioning allegiance to the racial quest for freedom and then re-

fusal to betray that quest to personal benefit or the diverting pursuit of lesser goals. Those who detour from the prescribed path are labeled "sell-outs," "traitors," or "Uncle Toms." . . .

The rhetoric of racial authenticity has been employed to reveal the ostensibly authentic bases of black intellectual and artistic expression. Those who deviate from familiar forms of racial identity and cultural expression are termed "oreos" or "incognegroes." (1993, xviii)

Reactions to Shelby Steele's book, *The Content of Our Character: A New Vision of Race Relations in America* (1990), crystalizes the racial ostracization of African American intellectuals whose discourse turns on the cult of personality. Steele argues that when blacks no longer see themselves as victims in their advancement into the mainstream middle class, they often see themselves as blameworthy—since the loss of victim status means a loss of racial innocence and their advancement as middle class makes them complicit in racism (1990, 14). But when looking at the disparity in the quality of life that binds inner-city communities today with black communities thirty years ago, Steele notes "residents feel less safe, drug trafficking is far worse, crimes by blacks against blacks are more frequent, housing remains substandard, and teenage pregnancy rate has skyrocketed" (14). He wonders to what extent these conditions ought to be structured under the rhetoric of racial innocence and victimization (15). "If conditions have worsened for most of us as racism had receded," he concludes, "then much of the problem must be of our own making. To admit this fully would cause us to lose the innocence we derive from our victimization" (15).

Steele's argument asserts a positive proposal that decenters racial community while privileging personality.

We must free our individuals from the tyranny of a wartime collectivism in which they must think of themselves as victims in order to identify with their race. The challenge now is to reclaim ourselves from the exaggerations of our own memory and to go forward as the free American citizens that we are. There is no magic that will make development happen. We simply have to want more for ourselves, be willing to work for it, and not use our enemy—old or new—as an excuse not to pursue it. (165)

Steele's book tends to provoke negative criticism because it proposes a politics of black identity that eschews those former racial projects that construe race under a forensic rhetoric. A forensic rhetoric judges and assigns innocence and guilt. Having become architectonic, Steele argues, forensic rhetoric ironically undermines the successful integration of African Americans into the cultural values and benefits of middle-class American citizenship. Displacing this racial rhetoric puts the critic not only at risk of racial irrelevance but also at risk of racial ostracism.

Steele's book has provoked a myriad of criticisms. Most are mixed, but the negative reviews are most revealing about the difficulties of promoting African American cultural criticism. Negative critiques tend to stress how those projects in African American cultural criticism that are predicated on the cult of personality constitute moral failure, a perversity of character, and a capitulation of the critic to market morality (notwithstanding traditional blaming the victims and Uncle Tomist retorts).

Patricia Williams is a critic who finds Steele's preoccupation with personality an aggrandizement of Steele's own personality, such that "when Steele's inner thoughts become externalize as 'our' world, some pretty reprehensible character traits get projected on 'us'" (1990, 12).

Constance Johnson reports for *U.S. News & World Report:*

Judging by the reviews, Shelby Steele is virtually a traitor to his race. Steele, . . . has been denounced in recent months for writing "a feel good manual for whites" (former Jesse Jackson campaign advisor Ronald Walters), for providing "comfort to whites" (civil rights leader Roger Wilkins) and for being "the latest black conservative discovered by the white media" (National Association for the Advancement of Colored People Executive Director Benjamin Hooks). (42)

To the list of racially ostracized critics, Johnson adds Thomas Sowell, Glenn Loury, Walter Williams, and William Julius Wilson. All of these critics, Johnson says, "have also been denounced as neo-conservatives and apologists for the white establishment" (42).

Writing in *Time*, Sylvester Monroe reports that critics like Steele, Loury, and Sowell are primary targets of racial castigation. He cites "Martin Kilson, Harvard's first black tenure professor: 'Steele's stuff is simpleminded, one-dimensional psychological reductionism." Citing Benjamin Hooks, he says, "It's slick sophistry. These people have nothing to offer except a conservative viewpoint in a black skin" (1990, 45). So-called black neoconservative cultural critics are often dismissed as racially irrelevant because their critics see in their proposed cult of personality a moral failure.

Patricia Williams comments on Steele's book:

> His conclusions can only be understood within the model of private contract law, in which self-interested, right-thinking action becomes the credit limit on the moral claims each person can make on society. Mr Steele wrongly poses this private contract as the antithesis of black identity; for him, the way out of the inner-city "heart of darkness" is to place in opposition the one and the many, so that "individual effort within the American mainstream—rather than collective action against the mainstream" becomes "our means of advancement." (1990, 12)

If so-called black neoconservatives err in their cultural criticism on the side of personality, then critics who privilege racial loyalty and authenticity are also subject to criticisms of racial utopianism, ethnocentrism, and sometimes racism. Such critiques are often directed against revolutionary cultural Afrocentricity. Molefi Kete Asante explains *Afrocentricity* as a rhetorical invention in the critique of ideology. Asante advocates a trimodal understanding of criticism, which he describes as descriptive, programmatic, and pejorative (1987, 5). This trimodal characterization of criticism parallels the descriptive, pejorative, and positive qualities of the criticism that I outlined in chapter 1. Descriptively, Afrocentricity has a historical function in which those discourses produced by African American intellectuals, which are concerned with African culture and behavior, ought to be determined by African modes of speaking and understanding (6–7). This requires a historical reconstruction of African American self-consciousness and knowledge that is centered by an African worldview and African realities (9).

By accenting the need of African American scholars to center their discourse on an African worldview and African realities, Afrocentricity necessarily is a comparative ideology at the pejorative level of criticism. As a comparative project, Afrocentricity decenters Eurocentric modes of understanding by exposing the real interests of European intellectuals in justifying and maintaining European imperialist intentions in the cultural realities of Africa (9). Programmatically, Afrocentricity intends a transformation of African American self-consciousness that is capable of alleviating the devastating signs of cultural alienation that characterize African American life and experience as a consequence of European imperialist practices (1991, 134). Such signs are black nihilism, community fragility, and self-hatred.

The ultimate end of Afrocentric discourse is what Asante calls *transcendence*. Cultural transcendence is the personal and communal harmony that is mediated by the recovery of African modes of understanding nature and human relationships (1987, 181). Asante proposes that ancient Kemet is the place to begin the threefold ideological intentions of Afrocentricity:

> Afrocentric analysis re-establishes the centrality of the ancient Kemetic (Egyptian) civilization and the Nile Valley cultural complex as points of reference for an African perspective in much the same way as Greece and Rome serve as reference points for the European world. Thus, the Afrocentricist expands human history by creating a new path for interpretation. . . . African is identified with time, place, and perspective. Without the Afrocentric perspective the imposition of the European line as universal hinders cultural understanding and demeans humanity. (9–10)

Commenting on Molefi Asante's *Kemet, Afrocentricity, and Knowledge* (1990), one reviewer, Uzo Esonwanne, recognizes that African Americans have legitimate political interest in resisting imperialism as historic victims of its colonizing practices. And "because such solidarity is desirable," he says, "we should hold the temptation to dismiss the notion of Afrocentricity completely on abeyance" (1992, 206). But he also castigates *Kemet* as "a masterpiece in (dis)ingenuousness" (203). Asante's proposal is regarded as "blunt racial manicheism" and the adoption of "the mantle of African and African American heroes" (204). Esonwanne criticizes Asante's version of Afrocentricity as mirroring the very discourses Kemet and Afrocentricity are supposed to negate:

> So implausible is Asante's discussion of Kemet, Africa, epistemology, and research methods, so disorganized is his presentation of his argument, and so crude and garbled are his analysis of various philosophical movements and individual authors that one may be forgiven for dismissing the whole project of Afrocentrism out of hand or accusing him of causing incalculable harm to the serious study of African American and African cultures. Sometimes Kemet is so offhandedly racist as to take the readers breath away. In spite of these difficulties, however, Kemet does possess what I chose to call negative value. By this I mean that it is exem-

plary of the sort of conceptual, epistemological, and theological approaches to research that scholars involved in
African American and African Studies programs would do
well to avoid. This is the sense in which, in my view, it may
be said to have some intellectual value. (206)

Other critics of cultural Afrocentricity regard this movement
not only as a positive ideology insofar as it proposes a cultural
revolution. They also see it as uncritically racist in its preten-
tious mimicry of traditional African practices.

In his article, "Racism 101," Andrew Sullivan, reporting in
The New Republic, summarizes his orientation to the Second
National Conference on the Infusion of African and African
American Content in the High School Curriculum and its culminating event—"the Ashanti Enstoolment ceremony." The
event was held in November 1990 at the Mariott Marquis in
Atlanta. In order to appreciate fully Sullivan's repulsion toward
cultural Afrocentricity, his description of the event is worth
quoting at length:

> The major social event of the conference was the Ashanti
> Enstoolment ceremony, held in the Imperial Ballroom. An
> enstoolment is a mark of respect for an African elder—in
> this case John Henrik Clarke, a professor emeritus at
> Hunter College in New York—it involves an elaborate
> lowering of the man three times onto the seat of learning.
> The ceremony began with the blowing of a shell-horn and
> the beating of African drums. Professors and teachers pro-
> cessed in elaborate African costume; Jeffries held a stick
> aloft; young girls performed a beautiful barefoot dance. A
> minister poured water from a jug north, south, east and
> west. As he poured to the east, he asked the thousand or so
> in the audience to invoke the names of their ancestors. The
> names of "Marcus," "Malcolm," "Elijah Muhammed," rang
> through the hall. "Ancestors, reclaim us, rename us, in At-
> lanta, in diaspora," intoned the minister.

A woman in a large headdress came on the stage: "May I ask the elders for permission to speak?" They gave permission. "Good evening," she said to the crowd, who responded meekly. "Now we can do better than that," she retorted, reminding us that this was after all, a conference of high school teachers. Then five bare-chested men in sashes, with gold bangles around their heads, paraded in, carrying a vast yellow parasol topped by a small ivory elephant. Underneath: a large stern woman, apparently the "queen mother," and, behind her, the diminutive Clarke, dressed in a suit and tie. Jeffries ranted for a while on the podium: "Education is not just about passing exams to get a job. It's about moving forward and tapping into our ancestors." We then recited a pledge: "We, the African community, in the hells of North America, do pledge our minds, our selves, and our bodies to further the struggle . . . because the work that we Africans have to do is the work of eternity, the work of the pyramid builders."

There was something about the event that finally began to sicken. It started with expensive costumes of the predominantly middle-class crowd. It continued with some of the points already made that day: that ancient Egypt was uniformly a black African culture, that no Semitic peoples were involved in the building of the pyramids, that no Jews were enslaved in Egypt, that Western philosophy was "vomit"—and the ingenuousness with which such ideas were received. It culminated in Clarke's assertion that no black American should soil herself with Christianity: "at what point do we stop the mental prostitution to a religion invented by foreigners? All religion is artificial. All major religions of the world are male chauvinist murder cults. (21)

Sullivan's description of this *enstoolment* ceremony highlights the performative absurdities that follow when cultural Afrocentrists attempt to act on radicalized tenets of Afrocentricity. Not only are the experiences of African American cultural life dis-

torted in the dramatized acts of the ceremony, but African traditional religions and cultures are themselves distorted by such a
performance. Like other critics of cultural Afrocentricity, Sullivan is not unsympathetic to the need for education that will
inspire racial pride and esteem—such aims seem fair enough.
But he sees in much of the rhetoric that structures this event a
mirroring of the racial intolerance, dogmatism, and misunder-
standings that historically have justified African imperialism
and its racist practices (21).

Professor Carmen Braun Williams also worries that the positive value of Afrocentricity is becoming more and more intoler-
ant of the difference included in African American cultural life
in the United States. At a meeting of the Association of Black
Psychologists in Ocho Rios, Jamaica, in 1990, Williams recounts
her disappointment with a panelist who was responding to a
question from the floor concerning the status of homosexuals
in the Afrocentric agenda. In the name of Afrocentricity, the
panelist outwardly condemned African American homosexual-
ity as "(1) abhorred among African peoples, (2) inconsistent
with African values, and (3) a 'white' disease that all African
Americans must reject" (1992, 46).

Williams goes on to say that "I thought this panelist's folly
would be apparent. Yet, to my surprise and disappointment,
around the room, many were nodding with agreement" (46).
Williams also notes that too many of the critiques against those
who would challenge such assumptions in the name of a
broader humanism are quickly dismissed as "betraying the race"
by persistently advocating "Eurocentric" values of "self-reliance
as a strategy for community development" (46). She warns that
"we must take caution that we do not, in our urgency to fill a
void and experience wholeness, engage in a love affair that
idolizes its object but refuses to recognize its flaws. Just as we
must reject Eurocentric models that oppress us, we must also
separate what is limiting about Afrocentricity from what is liberating" (46).

The two scenarios discussed above—black neoconservative discourse and cultural Afrocentricity—reveal two levels at which African American religious critics risk irrelevance in the contemporary context of cultural criticism. First, when proffering moral rhetorics such as community, unity, racial pride, and black interests, such languages tend to mitigate whatever claims critics also want to make for difference. The community for which such rhetoric is supposed to reassure is fraught with interests that are not always compatible with the nebulous totality of race. Second, those critics whose point of departure is *personality* have a difficult time justifying the claims that they want to make for community, while at the same time privileging self-realization at the levels of labor, family, gender, sexual interests, and personal lifestyle choices that center on the freedom of movement between inner-city, suburban, and rural communities.

Negotiating the two categories of community and personality with intellectual, political, and moral integrity locates the intellectual crisis of African American cultural and religious criticism, says Cornel West:

> One reason quality leadership is on the wane in black America is the gross deterioration of personal, familial, and communal relations among African-Americans. These relations—though always fragile and difficult to sustain—constitute a crucial basis for the development of a collective and critical consciousness and a moral commitment to and courageous engagement with causes beyond that of one's self and family. Presently, black communities are in shambles, black families are in decline, and black men and women are in conflict (and sometimes combat). In this way, the new class divisions produced by black inclusion (and exclusion) from the economic boom and the consumerism and hedonism promoted by mass culture have resulted in new kinds of personal turmoil and existential meaninglessness in Black

America. There are few, if any, communal resources to help black people cope with this situation. (1993, 36–37)

To conclude, critics such as Adolph Reed, bell hooks, and Cornel West propose a need for a form of criticism that goes beyond ontological blackness. In politics, Reed proposes that when the critical issues of African American public life turn on political representation and appropriate political strategies, critics need to attend to electoral mechanisms that ground representation no longer in terms of organic legitimacy but on "public validation at regular intervals." Reed also argues that "organic representation sidesteps the problems of validation by assuming automatically that the interests of representatives and constituents are identical" (1986, 124). The rationales undergirding Reed's proposal for cultural transcendence are grounded on the prospects of actualizing democratic practices among a politically informed and activated African American citizenry. The cultivation of racial transcendence among African Americans requires "a spirit of civic liberalism in Afro-American politics," says Reed (134). An African American politics that goes beyond ontological blackness may be legitimately procedural (based on rational-discursive principles) if not organic (135).

The position taken by both hooks and West on the prospects of racial transcendence points to an advancement of an insurgency model of discourse. Their model is predicated on an unrelenting commitment to the politics of difference, says hooks (1990, 16ff.). West has recently attempted to capture the connotations of such a discourse under the sign of "Race-Transcending Prophetic Criticism." "To be a serious black leader," West contends, "is to be a race-transcending prophet who critiques the powers that be (including the black component of the Establishment) and who puts forward a vision of moral regeneration and political insurgency for the purpose of fundamental social change for all who suffer from socially induced misery" (1993, 46).

Race-transcending prophetic criticism remains avant-garde insofar as the critic is committed intellectually to "grasping the structural and institutional processes that have disfigured, deformed, and devastated black America such that the resources for nurturing collective and critical consciousness, moral commitment, and courageous engagement are vastly underdeveloped" (1993, 45). However, race-transcending prophetic criticism is not avant-garde insofar as "the time has past for black political and intellectual leaders to pose as the voice for black America," says West (46).

These thinkers may differ on how the legitimate public role of the African American intellectual in public life is to be construed. But what their criticisms share is an iconoclastic rigor that is at the same time utopian. For these critics, the stereoscopic gaze that keeps both eyes open in the critique of black life and experience is the normative gaze of African American cultural and religious criticism. However, the positive challenge of postmodern blackness is to free up religious discourse from the essentialized burdens of racial representation/racism so that African American theology may be freed up to contribute positively to a new politics of black identity. Such a theology will take seriously the ethnic, class, gender, and sexual differentials that structure contemporary African American public life. And the grotesque qualities of African American contemporary life require grotesque symbols that reflexively disclose the complexities of African American public life.

Taking its cues from the iconoclastic and utopian dispositions of religious criticism, African American theology will support the categorical and reflexive goods that African American people require minimally for a life of struggle and survival. But it will ultimately intend a life of thriving, flourishing, and cultural fulfillment. The public burden of African American theology is to participate relevantly in the grotesque character of African American life. Carrying out this task will not be easy; for postmodern blackness has put African American theology in a crisis of legitimation. As African American theologians deliberate on the legitimation crisis of public theology in North America, cynicism and uncritical optimism are both out of order. What is warranted is a healthy pessimism about the fragility of our efforts to transcend absolutely cultural activities that threaten cultural fulfillment and a pragmatic hope that discerns and supports those activities that bring about more fulfillment of basic human needs and subjective goods.

By operationalizing these iconoclastic and utopian critical dispositions, African American theology (like African American literary and cultural criticism) will be freed up from ontological blackness to play in the grotesquery of both postmodern blackness and postmodern North American life.

EPILOGUE

■ ■ ■

It is a diagnosis of our times that the public relevancy of theology is in a crisis of legitimation. And the public crisis of American theology is often spoken of as a crisis of intellectual leadership. The public relevancy of theology is no longer carried out in a climate of ecclesiastical ecumenism and its theologically liberal justifications. It was this climate that gave great specificity to Howard Thurman's philosophy of religion and his message of universal reconciliation. His vision of reconciliation entails both harmony between the world's religions and races in the interest of a world community.

Our context is one that is circumscribed by the marginalization of mainline denominationalism in world affairs. The World Council of Churches is not likely to affect world politics, ethnic purging, or resurgent nationalisms throughout the world. And the resurgent interest in globalization in recent theological discussions also appears as the specter of ecumenical hope, but it lacks the power of a viable unifying theology, as Protestant liberalism once provided past American public theologies.

The ascendancy of so-called postliberal theologies in much of contemporary theological education today announces the end of ecumenical theology and its optimistic hope for public theology. Yet postliberal options are equally caught in the impasses of our cultural crises. Among many academic theologians, there is a growing entrenchment of the theological discipline. The new Yale theology of Hans Frei and George Lindbeck and the narrative theology and ethics of John Howard Yoder and Stanley Hauerwas appear preoccupied with doctrinaire, communitarian interests such as the preservation of particular church doctrines and ecclesiastical practices in the interest of religious identity formation. Postliberal and narrative theologies offer churches and their theologians valuable resources for the maintenance of ecclesiastical identity. But their communitarian interests are not likely to ameliorate the social problems that bind American public life.

American public life is a battleground of conflicting religious ideologies, all of which are supported by appeals to some defining faith narrative about America's meaning (Hunter, 1991, 42ff.). The loss of any grand metanarratives among the competing religious options makes narrative theology and ethics an unlikely candidate for a viable public theology. If these projects are concerned with religious identity formation, their prospects for success are promising. But the concern of public theology is public relevancy, and here not much is expected to change under the impetus of these reentrenching theologies.

The crisis of theology that I have briefly described above is not peculiar to ecumenical and postliberal theologies in predominantly white universities, divinity schools, and seminaries. African American theology has not been any more effective than these other theologies in the political life of African Americans. Those grand projects that propose liberation intentions also continue to mirror the dead ends of those theologies that justify themselves as crisis and existential theologies. The black theology project attempted a grand synthesis when it proposed the union of Marxism with the existential theology of Karl Barth and Paul Tillich in the interests of a theology of black self-consciousness. The synthesis has not been successful.

The first decade of the black theology project found African American theologians preoccupied with reconstructing theological methodology in terms of hermeneutics and rewriting

Christian theology from the perspective of black life and experience (ontological blackness). Black life and experience were described as the totality of black suffering and survival against the dehumanizing effects of white racism. Black suffering and survival became not only formal marks of ontological blackness, but also the substantive content of black theology; it is a fundamental symbol of the black theologian's ultimate concern.

The identification of ontological blackness with *ultimate concern* leaves black theology without the hope of cultural transcendence from the blackness that whiteness created. Consequently, black liberation is reduced to the development of a positive racial consciousness that renews black men and women for the defense of black humanity. But black theology remains an existential theology since its primary interest is in identity formation and explicating authentic forms of consciousness. But whatever claims are made for its revolutionary intentions to bring about the amelioration of African American social life remain unfulfilled.

There is a need for an African American public theology that goes beyond black crisis and existential theology. *Beyond Ontological Blackness* is for me a platform from which to clear a critical path for a more constructive work on African American public theology. Such a theology will require resources from a wide variety of fields. It will also seek to get beyond prior preoccupations with existential hermeneutics and its racial politics that have controlled the productions of African American theology until recently. Such a theology will seek to explicate the content of liberation not only in terms of positive self-consciousness at the various levels in which African American life is lived: class, ethnicity, gender, and sexual orientation. It will also place itself at the risk of public irrelevancy when its emancipatory aims are tested within the often compromising realm of public policy. The risks to such a theology will be justified pragmatically by whatever contributions it can render toward the fulfillment of the cultural values that African Americans hold and require as citizens within a Western democratic society.

The word *beyond* in the title of this book does not suggest a negation of African American interests in the formation of communities where visions of human flourishing are fulfilled and civil rights are protected and supported. However, the iconoclastic and enlightening concerns of religious and cultural criticism make it important for African Americans to recognize even among ourselves demonic presences that render many members of our own communities pseudospecies.

When black identities are justified primarily in terms of ontological blackness, too many of the differences that genuinely signify black life and culture recede into the background. Too often the heroically representational qualities of racial genius, the cult of black masculinity, and its often brutal forms of conformity gain ascendancy. Idolatry is idolatry wherever it is found. African American religious and cultural criticism, if it is to be effectively descriptive, pejorative, and constructive, would do well to attend to the grotesque ways that African American life and culture present themselves. What we all seek is cultural fulfillment. It is this that motivates African American religious and cultural criticism. The quest for cultural fulfillment should also motivate African American public theology.

FURTHER READING

■ ■ ■

A literature is developing on the idea of race as a linguistic or conceptual invention rather than a category of metaphysical ontology. See Adalberto Aguirre, Jr., and David V. Baker, eds., *Sources: Notable Selections in Race and Ethnicity* (Guilford, Conn.: Dushkin Publishing Group, 1995); David Theo Goldberg, *Racist Culture: Philosophy and the Politics of Meaning* (Cambridge, Mass.: Blackwell, 1993); Cornel West, "A Genealogy of Modern Racism," in *Prophesy Deliverance* (Philadelphia: Westminster Press, 1982), 47–68; Anthony Appiah, "Race," in Frank Lentricchia and Thomas McLaughlin, eds., *Critical Terms for Literary Study* (Chicago: University of Chicago Press, 1990), 274–287.

Much of the ongoing research and debate on racial representation is occurring within African American literary and cultural criticism. Michelle Wallace's *Black Popular Culture*, Gina Dent, ed. (Seattle: Bay Press, 1992) is an exemplary collection of essays that emphasize the historical and contemporary debates on racial representation and essentialism among contemporary African American critics.

CHAPTER ONE:
The Religious Functions of Cultural Criticism

Besides works cited by Habermas, Schutz, and Luckmann, other important sources for the theory of cultural analysis that I develop in this book are Peter L. Berger and Thomas Luckmann, *The Social Construction of Reality* (New York: Doubleday, 1967) and Peter L. Berger, *The Sacred Canopy* (New York: Doubleday, 1969). Robert Wuthnow's *Meaning and Moral Order: Explorations in Cultural Analysis* (Berkeley: University of California Press, 1987) and Wuthnow et al., *Cultural Analysis: The Work of Peter L. Berger, Mary Douglas, Michel Foucault, and Jürgen Habermas* (Boston: Routledge, 1984) are important sources for cultural analysis. Several books apply the critical theory of Habermas to social theory and theology. See Russell Keat, *The Politics of Social Theory: Habermas, Freud, and the Critique of Positivism* (Chicago: University of Chicago Press, 1981), and Paul Lakeland, *Theology and Critical Theory: The Discourse of the Church* (Nashville: Abingdon, 1990); Peter C. Hodgson, "Transfigurative Praxis: Shapes of Freedom," in *God in History* (Nashville: Abingdon, 1989, 215–29, and see Hodgson's discussion of communicative rationality and communicative freedom in *Winds of the Spirit: A Constructive Christian Theology* (Louisville: Westminster John Knox Press, 1994), 130–32.

The so-called new natural law school informs my emphasis on substantive goods and cultural fulfillment. See Chapters 10 and 11, "The Constitution, Life, Liberty, and Justice" and "Theories of Ethics" in Germain Grisez and Joseph Boyle, Jr., *Life and Death with Liberty and Justice* (Notre Dame: University of Notre Dame Press, 1979), 298–380, and Grisez and Russell Shaw, chapter 2, "Free Choice, Self-Determination, Community, and Character," and chapter 5, "The Goods Which Fulfill Persons" in *Fulfillment in Christ: A Summary of Christian Moral Principles* (Notre Dame: University of Notre Dame Press, 1991); also Germain Grisez, Joseph Boyle, and John Finnis, "Practical Principles, Moral Truth, and Ultimate Ends," in John Finnis, ed., *Natural Law Volume I* (New York: New York University Press, 1992), 99–289.

Howard Thurman's bibliography is quite extensive and a large secondary literature has emerged on the life and thought of Thurman. Books by Howard Thurman include *The Creative Encounter* (Richmond: Friends United Press, 1954), *Jesus and the Disinherited* (Richmond: Friends United Press, 1976), *For the Inward Journey: The Writings of Howard Thurman* (Richmond: Friends United Press, 1984), and *The Inward Journey* (Richmond: Friends United Press, 1980). Among the secondary literature, see Luther E. Smith, "An American Prophet: A Critical Study of the Thought of Howard Thurman" (St. Louis: St. Louis University, dissertation, 1979) and *Howard Thurman: The Mystic as Prophet* (Washington: University Press of America, 1981); Lerone Bennett, Jr., "Howard Thurman: 20th Century Holy Man," *Ebony*, Feb. (1978); Mosella G. Mitchell, *Spiritual Dynamics of Howard Thurman's Theology* (Bristol, Ind.: Wyndam Hall Press, 1985), idem, ed. *The Human Search: Howard Thurman and the Quest for Freedom* (New York: Lang, 1992); Walker E. Fluker, *They Looked for a City: a Comparative Analysis of the Ideal of Community in the Thought of Howard Thurman and Martin Luther King, Jr.* (Washington: University Press of America, 1989).

Cornel West is developing an extensive bibliography, which includes among the works cited, *The Ethical Dimensions of Marxist Thought* (New York: Monthly Review Press, 1991); *Beyond Eurocentrism and Multiculturalism* (Monroe, Maine: Common Courage Press, 1993), and with James Snead, *White Screens, Black Images: Hollywood from the Dark Side* (London: Routledge, 1994).

A number of recent articles about West have also begun to surface. See "Black Politics, Black Leadership: An Interview with Cornel West," *Christian Century* 110/23, Aug. 11(1993): 774–77; Amy Hamilton, "Insurgent Black Intellectual Life," *Off Our Backs* 23/7, July(1993)1–3; Ellis Cose, "A Prophet with Attitude," *Newsweek* 121/23, June 7 (1993):71; Jack White, "Philosopher with a Mission," *Time* 141/23, June 7(1993):60–62; Jill Nelson, "Cornel West: Hopeful Critic," *Essence* 23/12, Apr.(1993):54; Jarvis Anderson, "The Public Intellectual," *New Yorker* 69/46, Jan. 17(1994):39–48; and "Cornel West," *Current Biography*. 54/10, Oct.(1993):51–54.

CHAPTER TWO:
Categorical Racism and Racial Apologetics

On the historical interstices of European aesthetics and African American cultural philosophy a number of important texts are available. See Martin Bernal, *Black Athena: The Afroasiatic Roots of Classical Civilization*, Volume 1: The Fabrication of Ancient Greece, chapters 6 and 7 "Hellenomania" (New Brunswick: Rutgers University Press, 1987), 281–336; Lawrence W. Levine, *Black Culture and Black Consciousness: Afro-American Folk Thought from Slavery to Freedom* (Oxford: Oxford University Press, 1977); Sterling Stuckey, *Slave Culture: Nationalist Theory and the Foundations of Black America*, (New York: Oxford University Press, 1987); Gina Dent, ed., *Black Popular Culture* (Seattle: Bay Press, 1992); Manning Marable, "Historical Prologue, Towards a General Theory of Black Politics," in *Black American Politics: From the Washington Marches to Jesse Jackson* (London: Verso, 1985), 1–73; Timothy E. Fulup, "The Future Golden Day of the Race: Millennialism and Black Americans in the Nadir, 1877–1901," *Harvard Theological Review* 84/1, (1991):75–99; Gerald Early, ed., *Lure and Loathing: Twenty Black Intellectuals Address W. E. B. Du Bois's Dilemma of the Double-Consciousness of African Americans* (New York: Penguin Books, 1994); Robert Michael Franklin, *Liberating Visions: Human Fulfillment and Social Justice in African-American Thought* (Minneapolis: Fortress, 1990); and Robert A. Hill, ed., "General Introduction," in *The Marcus Garvey and Universal Negro Improvement Association Papers* volume 1. (Berkeley: University of California Press, 1983), xxxv–xl.

CHAPTER THREE:
Ontological Blackness in Religion and Theology

Major contributions to the study of black religion are E. Franklin Frazier, *The Negro Church in America* (New York: Schocken Books, 1963); Joseph R. Washington, Jr., *Black Religion: The Negro and Christianity in the United States* (Boston: Beacon, 1964),idem, *The Politics of God* (Boston: Beacon, 1967); C. Eric Lincoln, *The Black Church Since Frazier* (New York: Schocken Books, 1974), idem, *Race, Religion, and the Continuing American Dilemma* (New York: Hill and Wang, 1984); Gayraud S. Wilmore, *Black Religion and Black Radicalism* (Maryknoll: Orbis, 1983); and Albert J. Raboteau, *Slave Religion: The Invisible Institution in the Antebellum South* (Oxford: Oxford University Press, 1978).

The black theology project has taken three bibliographical trajectories, adequately documented in Gayraud Wilmore and James H. Cone, two volumes, *Black Theology: A Documentary History* (Maryknoll: Orbis, 1993). Works by James H. Cone, Gayraud Wilmore, Major Jones, and J. Deotis Roberts characterize the classical trajectory. The second trajectory represents an Afrocentric and narrative turn in black theology. Dwight N. Hopkins and George Cummings, eds., *Cut Loose the Stammering Tongue: Black Theology in the Slave Narratives* (Maryknoll: Orbis, 1991); Julian Kunnie, *Models of Black Theology: Issues in Class, Culture, and Gender* (Valley Forge, Pa.: Trinity Press, 1994); Riggins R. Earl, Jr., *Dark Symbols, Obscure Signs: God, Self, and Community in the Slave Mind* (Maryknoll: Orbis, 1993); and Peter J. Paris, *The Spirituality of African Peoples: The Search for a Common Moral Discourse* (Minneapolis: Fortress, 1995).

The third trajectory in black theology is the emergence of womanist theology. Besides works cited by Cannon, Grant, Williams, also see Deloris Williams, *Sisters in the Wilderness: The Challenge of Womanist God-Talk* (Maryknoll: Orbis, 1993); Kelly Brown Douglas, *The Black Christ* (Maryknoll: Orbis, 1994); Cheryl J. Sanders, ed., *Living the Intersection: Womanism and Afrocentrism in Theology* (Minneapolis: Fortress, 1995); Marcia Y. Riggs, *Awake, Arise and Act: A Womanist Call for Black Liberation* (Cleveland: Pilgrim Press, 1994); Evelyn Brooks Higginbotham. *Righteous Discontent: The Women's Movement in the Black Baptist Churches 1880–1920* (Cambridge, Mass.: Harvard University Press, 1993). Also see Burt James Lowenberg and Ruth Bogin, eds., *Black Women in Nineteenth-Century American Life* (University Park: Pennsylvania State University Press, 1976); Audre Lorde, *Sister Outsider* (Trumansberg, N.Y.: Crossing Press, 1984); Paula Giddings, *When and Where I Enter: The Impact of Black Women on Race and Sex in America* (New York: Bantam Books, 1984), and Patricia Hill Collins, *Black Feminist Thought* (London: Routledge, 1991).

CHAPTER FOUR:
Explicating and Displacing Ontological Blackness

Several significant books and articles on the heroic and grotesque aesthetics inform this essay. See Immanuel Kant, *Critique of Judgment* (New York: Hafner, 1968); Carl Skrade, *God and the Grotesque* (Philadelphia: Westminster, 1974); Charles E. Scott, "The Question Turns on Ethics: Self-overcoming in Nietzsche's Genealogy of the Ascetic Ideal," in *The Question of Ethics* (Bloomington: University of Indiana Press, 1990); Gregory Vlastos, *Socrates: Ironist and Moral Philosopher* (Ithaca: Cornell University Press, 1991); Frederick Burwick and Walter Pape, eds., *Aesthetic Illusion: Theoretical and Historical Approaches* (Berlin: Walter de Gruyter, 1990); Allan H. Pasco, "Toppling from Mount Olympus: The Romantic Hero," in Stephen M. Oberhelman, Van Kelly, and Richard J. Golsan, eds., *Epic and Epoch: Essays in the Interpretation and History of a Genre* (Lubbock: Texas Tech University Press, 1994), 233–47; and Jacques Derrida, *The Archeology of the Frivolous* (Lincoln: University of

Nebraska Press, 1973), idem, "Spurs: Nietzsche's Styles" in *A Derrida Reader: Between the Blinds*, Peggy Kamuf, ed. (New York: Columbia University Press, 1991), 355–77, and Jacques Derrida, *Memoirs of the Blind: The Self-Portrait and Other Ruins* (Chicago: University of Chicago Press, 1993).

On the new literary critiques of African American cultural philosophy, see Henry Louis Gates, Jr., *The Signifying Monkey: A Theory of African-American Literary Criticism* (New York: Oxford University Press, 1988), idem, *Figures in Black: Words, Signs, and the Racial Self* (New York: Oxford University Press, 1987); Houston A. Baker, Jr., *The Journey Back: Issues in Black Literature and Criticism* (Chicago: University of Chicago Press, 1980); idem, *Modernism and the Harlem Renaissance* (Chicago: University of Chicago Press, 1987); Baker, Jr., and Redmond, Patricia, eds., *Afro-American Literary Study in the 1990s* (Chicago: University of Chicago Press, 1989); and bell hooks, *Ain't I A Woman: Black Women and Feminism* (Boston: South End Press, 1981).

Epilogue

Postliberal theology and ethics tend to cover two tracks, the one is doctrinal and the other is narrative. Representative works include Hans Frei, *The Eclipse of Biblical Narrative* (New Haven: Yale University Press, 1974), *Theology and Narrative: Selected Essays*, George Hunsinger and William Placher, eds., (New York: Oxford University Press, 1993); George A. Lindbeck, *The Nature of Doctrine: Religion and Theology in a Postliberal Age* (Philadelphia: Westminster Press, 1984); David H. Kelsey, *To Understand God Truly: What's Theological About A Theological School* (Louisville: Westminster/John Knox Press, 1992); John Howard Yoder, *The Politics of Jesus* (Grand Rapids: Eerdmans, 1972), idem, *The Priestly Kingdom: Social Ethics as Gospel* (Notre Dame: University of Notre Dame Press, 1984); Stanley Hauerwas, *The Peaceable Kingdom: A Primer in Christian Ethics* (Notre Dame: University of Notre Dame Press, 1983); Hauerwas and L. Gregory Jones, eds., *Why Narrative?: Readings in Narrative Theology* (Grand Rapids: Eerdmans, 1989); Ronald Thiemann, *Revelation and Theology: The Gospel as Narrated Promise* (Notre Dame: University of Notre Dame Press, 1985).

Narrative theology and ethics is becoming one of the most recognized voices in North American theology. Any future African American public theology will have to consider its influence.

WORKS CITED

■ ■ ■

Asante, Molefi Kete.
  1987.   *The Afrocentric Idea*. Philadelphia: Temple University Press.
  1990.   *Kemet, Afrocentricity and Knowledge*. Trenton, N.J.: Africa World Press.
  1991.   "Afrocentricity and the African-American Student: A Challenge." *The Black Collegian*, March/April: 132–35.

Baker, Jr., Houston.
  1980.   *The Journey Back: Issues in Black Literature and Criticism*. Chicago: University of Chicago Press.
  1984.   *Blues, Ideology, and African American Literary Criticism*. Chicago: University of Chicago Press.

Bloom, Allan.
  1991.   *The Republic of Plato*. New York: Harper.

Blumenberg, Hans
  1983.   *The Legitimacy of the Modern Age*. Cambridge: MIT Press.

Burwick, Frederick.
  1990.   "The Grotesque: Illusion vs. Delusion." *Aesthetic Illusion: Theoretical and Historical Approaches*. Frederick Burwick and Walter Pape, ed. Berlin: de Gruyter, 122–37.

Cannon, Katie.
  1988.   *Black Womanist Ethics*. Atlanta: Scholars Press.

Cassirer, Ernst.
  1951.   *The Philosophy of the Enlightenment*. Princeton: Princeton University Press.

Cone, James H.
1986.   *Speaking the Truth*. Grand Rapids: Eerdmans.
1989.   *Black Theology and Black Power*. New York: Harper/Collins.
1991.   *A Black Theology of Liberation*. Maryknoll: Orbis.

Copeland, Shawn M.
1993.   "Wading Through Many Sorrows." Emilie Townes, ed. *A Troubling in My Soul: Womanist Perspectives on Evil and Suffering*. Maryknoll: Orbis, 109–29.

Douglas, Kelly Brown.
1994.   *The Black Christ*. Maryknoll: Orbis.

Dubey, Mahdu.
1994.   *Black Women Novelists and the Nationalist Aesthetic*. Bloomington: University of Indiana Press.

Du Bois, W. E. B.
1972.   *The Crisis Writings*. Daniel Walden, ed. Greenwich, Conn.: Fawcett.
1982.   *The Souls of Black Folk*. New York: New American Library.

Dyson, Michael Eric.
1993.   *Reflecting Black: African American Cultural Criticism*. Minneapolis: University of Minnesota Press.

Erikson, Erik H.
1968.   *Identity, Youth and Crisis*. New York: Norton.

Esonwanne, Uzo.
1992.   "Kemet, Afrocentricity and Knowledge." Book review. *Research in African Literatures*, 23/1:203–7.

Evans, James H.
1992.   *We Have Been Believers: An African American Systematic Theology*. Minneapolis: Fortress.

Fields, Barbara.
1990.   "Slavery, Race and Ideology in the United States of America." *New Left Review*, 181: 95–118.

Finnis, John, ed.
1992.   *Natural Law:* volume 1. New York: New York University Press.

Garvey, Marcus.
1983.   *The Marcus Garvey Papers and the Universal Negro Improvement*

Association Papers. vols. 1, 2, 5. Robert A. Hill, ed. Berkeley: University of California Press.

Gates, Jr., Henry Louis.
1992.   *Loose Canons: Note on the Culture Wars.* New York: Oxford University Press.

Geertz, Clifford.
1964.   "Ideology as Cultural System." David Apter, ed. *Ideology and Discontent.* New York: Free Press, 47–72.
1973.   *The Interpretation of Cultures.* New York: Basic Books.

Geuss, Raymond.
1981.   *The Idea of a Critical Theory: Habermas and the Frankfort School.* Cambridge: Cambridge University Press.

Goldberg, David Theo.
1993.   *Racist Culture: Philosophy and the Politics of Meaning.* Oxford: Blackwell.

Grant, Jacquelyn.
1989.   *White Women's Christ and Black Women's Jesus.* Atlanta: Scholars Press.

Grisez, Germain, and Shaw, Russell.
1991.   *Fulfillment in Christ: A Summary of Christian Moral Principles.* Notre Dame: University of Notre Dame Press.

Habermas, Jürgen.
1981.   "Modernity versus Postmodernity." *New German Critique,* 22:3–14.
1987.   *The Philosophical Discourse of Modernity.* Cambridge: MIT Press.
1989.   *Theory of Communicative Action.* Vol. 2. Boston: Beacon Press.

Hart, William D.
1994.   "Religion and its Secular Other." Princeton: Princeton University dissertation.

Hegel, G. W. F.
1952.   *Philosophy of Right.* Translated by T.M. Knox. London: Oxford University Press.

Hine, Darlene Clark.
1993.   "In the Kingdom of Culture: Black Women and the Intersection of Race, Gender, and Class." *Lure and Loathing: Twenty*

Black Intellectuals Address W.E.B. Du Bois's Dilemma of the Double-Consciousness of African Americans, Gerald Early, ed. New York: Penguin Group, 337–51.

hooks, bell.
 1981. *Ain't I A Woman: black women and feminism.* Boston: South End Press.
 1990. *Yearnings: Race, Gender, and Cultural Politics.* Boston: South End Press.

hooks, bell, and West, Cornel.
 1991. *Breaking Bread: Insurgent Black Intellectual Life.* Boston: South End Press.

Hopkins, Dwight.
 1993. *Shoes that Fit Our Feet: Sources for a Constructive Black Theology.* Maryknoll: Orbis.

Hunter, James Davidson.
 1991. *Culture Wars: The Struggle to Define America.* New York: Basic Books.

Huyssen, Andreas.
 1986. *After the Great Divide: Modernism, Mass Culture, Postmodernism.* Bloomington: University of Indiana Press.

Jameson, Frederic.
 1991. *Postmodernism or the Cultural Logic of Late Capitalism.* Durham: Duke University Press.

Jefferson, Thomas.
 1970. "Notes on the State of Virginia." *Great Documents in Black American History.* George Ducas and Charles Van Doren, eds. New York: Praeger, 14–21.

Jennings, Theodore W.
 1985. *The Vocation of the Theologian.* Philadelphia:Fortress.

Johnson, Constance.
 1990. "The Hidden Perils of Racial Conformity." *U.S. News & World Report,* Dec. 24. 109: 42–43.

Kant, Immanuel.
 1960. *Observations on the Feeling of the Beautiful and Sublime.* John T. Goldthwait, trans. Berkeley: University of California Press.

Kaufman, Gordon.
　1993.　　*In Face of Mystery*. Cambridge: Harvard University Press.

King, Jr., Martin Luther.
　1986.　　*A Testament of Hope: The Essential Writings of Martin Luther King, Jr.* James M. Washington, ed. New York: HarperCollins.

Lincoln, C. Eric.
　1993.　　"The Du Boisean Dubiety and the American Dilemma." *Lure and Loathing*, Gerald Early, ed. New York: Penguin Group, 194–206.

Lincoln, C. Eric, and Mamiya, Lawrence.
　1990.　　*The Black Church in the African American Experience*. Durham: Duke University Press.

Lyotard, Jean-François.
　1984.　　*The Postmodern Condition*. Minneapolis: University of Minnesota Press.
　1992.　　*The Postmodern Explained*. Minneapolis: University of Minnesota Press.

MacIntyre, Alasdair.
　1988.　　*Whose Justice? Which Rationality?* Notre Dame: University of Notre Dame Press.

Martin, Clarice.
　1993.　　"Black Women's Spiritual Autobiography." *A Troubling in My Soul: Womanist Perspectives on Evil and Suffering*. Maryknoll: Orbis, 13–36.

Mead, George Herbert.
　1932.　　*The Philosophy of the Present*. Chicago: University of Chicago Press.
　1964.　　*Select Writings: George Herbert Mead*. Chicago: University of Chicago Press.

Mehta, Uday S.
　1990.　　"Liberal Strategies of Exclusion." *Politics and Society*, 18/4: 427–55.

Monroe, Sylvester.
　1990.　　"Up from Obscurity." *Time*, Aug. 13, 136/7:45.

Morrison, Toni.
　1984.　　"Rootedness: The Ancestors as Foundation." Mari Evans, ed.

              Black Women Writers (1950–1980): A Critical Evaluation. Garden City, N.Y.: Anchor Press, 339–45.

1988.   "Unspeakable Things Spoken: The Afro-American Presence in American Literature." *Michigan Quarterly Review,* 28/1: 1–34.

1992.   *Playing in the Dark: Whiteness and the Literary Imagination.* New York: Vintage Books.

Moses, Wilson J.
1993.   "Ambivalent Maybe." *Lure and Loathing.* Gerald Early, ed. New York: Penguin Group, 274–90.

Murray, Albert.
1970.   *The Omni-Americans: Black Experience and American Culture.* New York: Da Capo Press.

Nietzsche, Friedrich.
1956.   *The Birth of Tragedy.* Garden City: Doubleday.
1974.   *The Gay Science.* Vintage Books.
1990.   *Twilight of the Idols.* New York: Penguin Books.

Oberhelman, Stephen M., Kelly, Van, and Golsan, Richard, eds.
1994.   *Epic and Epoch: Essays on the Interpretation and History of a Genre.* Lubbock: Texas Tech University Press.

Omi, Michael and Winant, Howard.
1995.   "Racial Formations in the United States from 1960s to the 1980s." *Sources: Notable Selections in Race and Ethnicity.* Adalberto Aguirre, Jr. and David V. Baker, eds. Guilford: Conn.: Dushkin Publishing Group, 3–13.

Paris, Peter J.
1985.   *The Social Teachings of the Black Churches.* Philadelphia: Fortress.

Popkins, Richard.
1977–78. "Hume's Racism." *Philosophical Forum,* 9/2–3: 211–26.

Quint, David.
1993.   *Epic and Empire: Politics and Generic Form from Virgil to Milton.* Princeton: Princeton University Press.

Rampersad, Arnold.
1990.   *The Art and Imagination of W. E. B. Du Bois.* New York: Schocken.

Reed, Jr., Adolph L.
　1986.　*The Jesse Jackson Phenomena: The Crisis of Purpose in Afro-American Politics.* New Haven: Yale University Press.

Rejai, Mostafa.
　1973.　"Ideology." *Dictionary of the History of Ideas.* Vol. 2. New York: Scribner's Sons, 552–59.

Rorty, Richard.
　1989.　*Contingency, Irony and Solidarity.* Cambridge: University of Cambridge Press.

Said, Edward.
　1979.　*Orientalism.* New York: Vintage Books.
　1983.　*The World, the Text, and the Critic.* Cambridge: Harvard University Press.
　1993.　*Culture and Imperialism.* New York: Knopf.

Sanders, Cheryl J.
　1989.　"Roundtable Discussion: Christian Ethics and Theology in Womanist Perspective." *Journal of Feminist Studies in Religion,* 5:83–91.

Schutz, Alfred, and Luckmann, Thomas.
　1973.　*The Structures of Life-Worlds.* Richard Zaner and H. T. Engelhardt, trans. Evanston: Northwestern University Press.

Shklar, Judith N.
　1991.　*American Citizenship: The Quest for Inclusion.* Tanner Lectures. Cambridge, Mass.: Harvard University Press.

Sigelman, Lee, and Welch, Susan.
　1991.　*Black Americans' Views of Racial Inequality: The Dream Deferred.* Cambridge: Cambridge University Press.

Steele, Shelby.
　1990.　*The Content of Our Character: A New Vision of Race Relations in America.* New York: Harper.

Stout, Jeffrey L.
　1988.　*Ethics after Babel: The Languages of Morals and Their Discontent.* Boston: Beacon Press.

Sullivan, Andrew.
　1990.　"Racism 101: A Crash Course in Afrocentricity." *The New Republic,* Nov. 26, 203: 18–21.

Thomson, Philip.
    1972.   *The Grotesque*. London: Methuen.

Thurman, Howard.
    1986.   *The Search for Common Ground*. Richmond: Friends United Press.

Tillich, Paul.
    1967.   *Systematic Theology*. Chicago: University of Chicago Press.

Tonelli, Giorgio.
    1973.   "Genius from the Renaissance to 1770." *Dictionary of the History of Ideas*. Vol. 2. New York: Scribner's Sons, 293–97.

Walker, David.
    1970.   "Appeal, in four Articles, together with a Preamble to the Colored Citizens of the World, but in Particular, and very Expressly to those of the United States." *Great Documents in Black American History*. George Ducas and Charles Van Doren, eds. New York: Praeger, 57–105.

Washington, Booker T.
    1974.   *The Booker T. Washington Papers*. Vol. 3. Louis R. Harlan, ed. Urbana: University of Illinois Press.
    1975.   *The Booker T. Washington Papers*. Vol. 4. Louis R. Harlan, ed. Urbana: University of Illinois Press.

Washington, Booker T., and Du Bois, W. E. B.
    1970.   *The Negro in the South*. New York: Citadel Press.

Washington, James M., ed.
    1986.   "Editor's Introduction: Martin Luther King, Jr., Martyred Prophet for a Global beloved Community of Justice, Faith, and Hope," in *A Testament of Hope*. New York: HarperCollins Publishers.

West, Cornel.
    1982.   *Prophesy Deliverance! An Afro-American Revolutionary Christianity*. Philadelphia: Westminster Press.
    1988.   *Prophetic Fragments*. Grand Rapids: Eerdmans.
    1989.   *The American Evasion of Philosophy*. Madison: University of Wisconsin Press.
    1993.   *Keeping Faith: Philosophy and Race in America*. New York: Routledge.

Williams, Carmen Braun.
    1992.   "Afrocentricity: Do or Die?" *Essence*, 23/8: 146.

Williams, Delores.
    1993.   "A Womanist Perspective on Sin." *A Troubling in My Soul: Womanist Perspectives on Evil and Suffering.* Maryknoll: Orbis, 130–50.

Williams, Patricia J.
    1990.   "A Kind of Race Fatigue." *New York Times Book Review*, Sept. 16. Sec. 7/1:12.

Wilmore, Gayraud.
    1983.   *Black Religion and Black Radicalism.* Maryknoll: Orbis.

Wilson, William Julius.
    1978.   *The Declining Significance of Race.* Chicago: University of Chicago Press.

INDEX

• • •